Bluffer's®

GUIDE TO

CHOCOLATE

D0809867

NEIL DAVEY

© Haynes Publishing 2018
Published June 2018

A CIP Catalogue record for this book
is available from the British Library.

ISBN: 978 1 78521 246 8

Library of Congress control no. 2018932893

Published by Haynes Publishing,
Sparkford, Yeovil, Somerset BA22 7JJ
Tel: 01963 440635
Int. tel: +44 1963 440635
Website: www.haynes.com

Printed in Malaysia.

Series Editor: David Allsop.
Front cover illustration by Alan Capel.

CONTENTS

If there's one food item that can really lay claim to being the food of love, it's chocolate.

THE FOOD OF LOVE

Shakespeare once suggested that music was the food of love. These days, chocolate has a powerful claim to having usurped it as the new food of love – not to mention the new black, the new Friday, the new 50, the new 80 and the new rock 'n' roll as well.

It all started with the sexing up of food itself. A few years ago, you were a genius if you could mix up a prawn cocktail sauce and translate half a dozen items on a French menu. These days, even if you own only a kettle and a toaster, many people still expect you to be able to rustle up something to inspire Gordon Ramsay, be fluent in 14 different menu languages, and be able to spot a ripe avocado at 20 paces.

A rudimentary knowledge of food is no longer socially acceptable. People do not simply ask you where you went on holiday; they want to know what and where you ate when you went on holiday, mostly so that they can ask if you visited that charming little deli in the old town that weaves its own tiramisu and crochets its own olive oil. People don't just want to know how long the beef was hung; they want to know the noble beast's name, its family tree, which field it was kept in and whether it was Jethro or his backward brother Silas who killed it. In the same way, they now want to know which bean has been used in the composition of your chocolate, and on which estate in which country it was grown, and when.

There could be many reasons why this sort of knowledge is now so desirable. Perhaps it sets you apart as a world traveller with an unquenchable curiosity and a wealth of fascinating experience behind you. Maybe it's just because it hints that you have a deep fund of knowledge about many things. Whatever the reason, there's one undeniable fact: it makes chocolate a wonderfully rich subject for the art of bluffing.*

It's cool, it's sexy, and it's available in myriad forms everywhere. It can be accessible or exclusive, cheap or expensive. It's produced all over the world and has a wealth of history behind it. It is said to possess all sorts of qualities, from aphrodisiac to energy booster. The process to turn it from bean to bar is fantastically complex. It is, therefore, the perfect food for the bluffer.

Over the next 120 pages or so you'll find everything you need to know to impress friends, family, colleagues, romantic interests, passing chefs and patronising waiters. Whether you're a regular consumer of French luxury chocolate Valrhona or if your knowledge begins and ends with a deep fried Mars Bar, you'll be able to hold your own in any chocolate-related situation. Even better, should you wish (for whatever reason) to do the additional research required without eating lots of different chocolate, this book will allow you to pontificate expertly without a crumb of the stuff passing your lips.

It sets out to conduct you through the main danger zones encountered in discussions about chocolate, and to equip you with a vocabulary and evasive technique that will minimise the risk of being rumbled as a bluffer. It will give you a few easy-to-learn hints and methods designed to ensure that you will be accepted as a chocolate aficionado of rare ability and experience.

But it will do more. It will provide you with the tools to impress legions of marvelling listeners with your knowledge and insight – without anyone discovering that, before reading it, you didn't know the difference between a bar of Fruit and Nut and an artisan micro-batch production of chocolate made from pure Criollo beans sourced from the Chuao plantation in Venezuela's Aragua valley. (Try to remember the latter part of that sentence, and quote it frequently – it's bluffing gold.)

*See *The Bluffer's Guide to Food*.

Ten cacao beans would secure the services of someone in – ahem – the world's oldest profession; it appears, then, that some people have always done anything for chocolate.

CHOCS AWAY

It's been a long and (often literally) tortuous route from the discovery of the cocoa bean to its packaging in purple wrapper and foil and ultimate sale in petrol stations. The complexities involved in the making of chocolate will be addressed in due course, as will the way it is wrapped.

At this point, it's enough to establish that we're talking about a particular product that can be made from the fruit of the cacao tree, a tree indigenous to the tropical climes of Central and South America. It is exactly the same as the cocoa tree but just that simple difference in spelling and pronunciation alone establishes you as someone with a greater depth of knowledge. As for when you should use cocoa/cacao to describe the product, the words are increasingly interchangeable. If you really want to impress, you can say that some conventions dictate that the beans are called cacao, while the powder that can be made from them is cocoa; but, in most cases, feel free to use either.

Leave the chocolate-making process until later and

let's start at the very beginning. The journey thus begins some 4,000 years ago with the Olmecs, the first major civilisation in what would later become Mexico.

It is perhaps worth pointing out here that, as with so much ancient history, there are contradictory dates and stories. For many, that would be frustrating. For the bluffer, though, such vagueness is manna from heaven. Even if you have a particularly vociferous expert desperately looking for the flaws in your story, you can laugh off their allegations with practised nonchalance and a well-placed 'Well, yes, according to some sources...' or 'I think the jury's still out on that one.'

THE OLMECS

According to some evidence, the Olmecs may have been the first civilisation in the Western Hemisphere to develop a system of writing. They're also said to have been the first to invent zero, calendars, bloodletting and human sacrifice; think of them as accountants gone bad. More importantly, they're thought to be the first known people to consume cacao beans, in around 600BC. The Aztecs and Mayans may have had chocolate bars named after them, but they came later. The Olmecs should probably have a word with their legal team about that.

The Olmecs were around from 1200BC until approximately 400BC – before dying out or moving on, possibly due to volcanic activity in the region or too many virgin sacrifices. Nobody's particularly sure what happened, but evidence suggests that they were the first to discover the delicious potential of the cacao bean: probably because their home was full of cacao trees, and excess is as much a mother of invention as necessity.

DRINKING CHOCOLATE

At this point, and for around the next two millennia, chocolate, or *xocoatl*, as certain records suggest it was called (don't even try to pronounce it), was consumed as a drink. It actually translates as 'bitter water' which doesn't make it sound terribly appetising – unless you're a fan of beer or Angostura, of course.

This is a point on which other experts may attempt to correct you, so be prepared. The American linguist William Bright argued that there's no evidence of *xocoatl* or *chocolatl* or any of the other possible spellings being used as a word at this time in history. It's possible, then, that our modern word comes from *chokol*, the Mayan word for 'hot', and *atl*, the word for 'water'. Others claim that the Aztec word *cacahuatl* ('cacao water') is the derivation. The latter has strong possibilities, particularly once the Spanish got involved. They'd have been unlikely – as anyone would – to have drunk a thick, brown liquid that had the word 'caca' in its name because, as any schoolboy knows, in Spanish that means 'poo' (or faecal matter if you're an adult). The theory, then, is that the Spanish substituted 'chokol' to make things somewhat more appetising.

For the sake of clarity, you'd probably be better sticking with the first version but do, of course, keep the others in your bluffing vocabulary. Drinking *xocoatl* (try pronouncing it 'hoch-co-atal' if you insist) was a practice that continued for many centuries – chocolate wasn't actually eaten in bar form until the nineteenth century – from the Mayans (when they weren't busy incorrectly predicting the end of the world) to the Aztecs and beyond.

THE MAYANS

The Mayans, as acknowledged by the Green & Black's bar named after them, were probably the first culture to fully embrace *xocoatl* and its health benefits. As the Mayans would have discovered, *xocoatl* was good for combating fatigue and as a stimulant in general. For the purposes of full pontificating, you may wish to note that there is a small amount of caffeine in the cacao bean but a greater amount of theobromine, a mild stimulant of the central nervous system that increases your serotonin levels; that's why eating chocolate makes you feel good.

The Mayans made *xocoatl* an integral part of their society and religion, a belief that continued with the Toltecs and the Aztecs, and even as far along as Carl von Linnaeus, the eighteenth-century Swedish scientist who gave the tree its Latin name, *Theobroma cacao*, which translates as 'food of the gods'. The Toltecs believed that cacao was a divine gift from the god Quetzalcoatl. Legend has it that Quetzalcoatl was banished by the other gods for giving man the gift of cacao, but had sworn to return. Remember that; it will come up again.

THE AZTECS

Next up, and also loving the bean, were the Aztecs. They had a mighty empire – some 15 million people between the fourteenth and sixteenth centuries – and held cacao in such high regard that the beans were used as currency, a practice that lasted in Central America until the nineteenth century. According to some contemporary accounts, a slave could be purchased for around 100 beans, four would get you a rabbit and around ten would secure the services of someone in – ahem – the world's oldest profession; it appears, then, that some people have always done anything for chocolate.

Because of the value of the beans, the drink was the privilege of the upper classes, with the Aztec emperor Montezuma II – who has also been remembered by the chocolate manufacturers of today – rumoured to consume up to 50 cups of *xocoatl* a day, often before visiting his harem of wives. Whether cacao works as a Viagra substitute is debatable – scientists have argued it both ways, and we'll take a look at that in a later chapter – but if it worked for Montezuma…

ARRIVAL IN EUROPE

Cacao became Montezuma's downfall in the incident that ultimately brought the bean to Europe. In 1519, Spanish explorer Hernán Cortés arrived in the Aztec capital Tenochtitlán and met with Montezuma. Montezuma was convinced that this exotic fellow, with his fairer skin and beard, had to be Quetzalcoatl returning from his banishment and thus showered the explorer with many gifts, including much-prized cacao. Giving this foreigner cacao was a decision that didn't go down well with Montezuma's people, who revolted and killed the emperor. As it happens, the masses were better judges of character than Montezuma as Cortés and the Spanish then went on to destroy most of the Aztec Empire.

Cortés brought cacao back to the Spanish court in 1527. Due to high taxes, once again the drink it made became the privilege of the upper classes, and less a mystery and more a complete secret as far as the rest of the world was concerned. According to some reports, Sir Francis Drake certainly had no idea what it was or its value; when he and his men captured Spanish galleons and discovered sacks full of cacao beans, they declared them useless and threw them overboard. Would the course of history have been different if they'd realised what their booty comprised? Would Drake and his men have returned to the Spanish Main to plunder more of the magic cacao beans, and would they have thus missed the bunfight with the Armada in 1588? Was Pope Sixtus V (who gave the Spanish aggressors his blessing) a Catholic? It's probably safe to say that Drake would have followed the money if only he'd known. These are all points for the bluffer to bear in mind in any discussion about the history of chocolate.

CHOCOLATE SPREADS

It wasn't until the seventeenth century that, with the marriage of Anne of Austria, daughter of Philip III of Spain, to Louis XIII of France, cacao started to spread across the rest of Europe. Around the same time, the medicinal properties of the drink had brought it to the attention of missionaries, and word spread across more of South and Central America and parts of Europe. Religion would also come to play a greater part in chocolate's evolution in the coming years.

Chocolate finally came to England – hurrah – in the mid-seventeenth century. Once again – you've guessed it – taxes meant that it was the rich who got to enjoy the drink. From 1657, chocolate houses sprang up across London as meeting places for the elite. Some of these, where men gathered to discuss politics and the pressing matters of the day over a cup of the brown stuff, later evolved into gentlemen's clubs.

INFLUENCE OF THE QUAKERS

For the next two centuries, chocolate remained as a drink famed for its various health benefits and mood-enhancing qualities. The fact that it did this without the presence of alcohol made it enormously attractive to the Quakers, something that would soon help shape the future of chocolate even further.

Because of their beliefs, Quaker career choices were somewhat limited, but medical professions were certainly permitted. Accordingly, many Quakers became doctors and apothecaries, and chocolate, with its famed/fabled health benefits, played a large part in their medicine chests. With the government reducing the import duty on cacao in the 1850s, and gin becoming increasingly popular among the population, the Quakers were also happy to have found something that they saw as a viable alternative to the demon drink. Three of the country's leading Quakers of the time were particularly eager to extol the virtues of this wonder substance. Their names? Prepare to be surprised: George Cadbury, Joseph Rowntree and Joseph Storrs Fry.

In 2011, the UK chocolate confectionery market was worth a little under £4 billion.

Beyond the products that still bear their names today, Cadbury, Rowntree and Fry made a vast contribution to British society. The high cost of chocolate meant that much of what had been sold before was adulterated with all sorts of alien substances – animal, vegetable and mineral. With the reduction in taxes and the Quaker involvement, that practice stopped.

The three Quakers also revolutionised working conditions. Cadbury created Bournville – the place (not the plain chocolate just yet) – as a utopia for his workers, swiftly followed by Rowntree and Fry, who gave their workers the best possible living and working conditions for the time. You could argue, then – or at least drop casually into the conversation – that chocolate has traditionally worked towards the common good and made people feel better in many ways beyond its physical effects.

GROWTH OF TECHNOLOGY

So, now there's a drink with certain health benefits, workers with better conditions than ever before, a dead emperor, extinct civilisations and the start of assorted men's clubs. What there isn't yet is something recognisable as a bar of chocolate. The stuff was still mainly in liquid form.

Around the same time that chocolate was gaining a foothold across Europe as a drink, things were happening that would take it to the form we know and love. A useful point to drop into conversations is just how much we consume. It changes from year to year but, according to the most recently available figures, in 2011 the UK chocolate confectionery market was worth a little under £4 billion.

Some key milestones were reached in the eighteenth and nineteenth centuries to take chocolate from a drink – and often a fatty, gritty drink at that – to the smoother, more refined chocolate that we drink and eat today.

Key to this was the invention of the cocoa press by Dutch chemist Conrad van Houten. When preparing chocolate, one of the problems people found was that cocoa butter rose to the top of the liquid, meaning that the drink had to be skimmed regularly or the fat had to be boiled off. Van Houten wanted to find a better way to remove this fat. It was a fine idea but it wasn't a quick process; van Houten began his research in 1815 but it wasn't until 1828 that he finally figured out what was going on and subsequently patented his invention.

The van Houten press separated the fat from the

chocolate liquor – we'll come to that in due course, but it's basically pure chocolate in its liquid form – leaving what we know as cocoa powder. Van Houten added potash to the powder, which made it darker in appearance, easier to mix and reduced the bitterness, giving the cocoa a milder flavour. This process, the alkalisation of cocoa, is still known today as 'Dutching' – possibly not the memorial van Houten was expecting, but at least it's a small acknowledgement, and he's still doing better than the Olmecs.

Thanks to the Dutching process, the famed chocolate drink could now be made more easily – and better tasting – just by adding water. It could also be produced on a grand scale, reducing the costs and making it accessible to everyone. It also led to the first 'modern' chocolate bar in 1847, courtesy of Joseph Fry.

By blending powdered cocoa with cocoa butter and sugar, Fry found that you could make a paste that could be easily shaped. Before this discovery, chocolate bars had existed but they needed to be dissolved in milk or water before they could be consumed. Fry's breakthrough was a bar you could eat without any further treatment. His reward – despite giving his bar the unwieldy name of *'chocolat délicieux à manger'* – was to see his company become the world's largest chocolate manufacturer.

It wasn't just in Britain and Holland where chocolate technology was leaping forward. The reason the Swiss are so often associated with fine chocolate today is down to their influence around the same time, particularly in the field of chocolate production.

While Fry discovered a method of mixing ingredients to make bars by hand, the Swiss found a way to do it by machine. The piece of equipment that combines cocoa paste and sugar into a smooth blend is known as a *mélangeur* and the invention is credited to Philippe Suchard. You might recognise the name.

The creation of milk chocolate – in 1875 – is also credited to the Swiss. It's made by adding powdered milk to the cocoa mixture and, interestingly, it's the chemist who worked out how to powder milk that is remembered rather than the chocolate maker who combined the ingredients for the first time. The chocolate maker was Swiss, one Daniel Peter. You might not recognise the name, but you may be more familiar with that of his German head chemist – Henri Nestlé. In the same year, Fry's also launched its remoulded cream-filled bar (orginally created in 1866), a definite acquired-taste product that is still available today.

Also in the same year, another Swiss man with a familiar name, Rodolphe Lindt, discovered 'conching'. All bluffers need to be aware of this step change in the production of chocolate, and it will be discussed at length in the next chapter. For now, all you need to know is that it's basically the process where chocolate loses its natural graininess and becomes the smooth, creamy product we know and buy so much of today. According to chocolate-making legend, Lindt discovered the process and the benefits of conching completely by accident when an employee left a machine running overnight.

Tasting chocolate is all a matter of confidence. It's your palate, so it's your rules.

MAKE IT AND BREAK IT

Now that terms such as 'conching' have cropped up, this might be a very good time to step away from the history and admire how the long, elaborate process of chocolate making has evolved. There is, after all, a big difference between the original drink and the modern bar. For the drink, it's a case of grinding down the seeds of the cacao plant and adding milk or water to make a fatty, gritty beverage. For the bar, it's a case of building a specialist machine to grind down the beans in a particular way, adding assorted ingredients, stirring it continuously for ten hours, spreading it back and forth on a cold piece of granite and keeping its temperature to about 32°C. It's a remarkable achievement that should be properly celebrated and, of course, discussed at length with an appropriate sense of gravitas, courtesy of your newly learned vocabulary.

This chapter is going to be information-heavy, but the forthcoming knowledge:

a) is a vital part of our subject;

b) will give you the ability to discuss chocolate with the desired air of nonchalance; and

c) perhaps best of all, will give you the vocabulary, wisdom and expertise to be able to pass judgement on all future chocolate you consume.

HOW IT'S MADE

Knowing how chocolate is made – in theory, obviously, not in practice, because that seems like an awful lot of work – puts you in an admirable position of authority, enabling you to break and sample bars and declare with confidence that the beans weren't dried enough or that the chocolate wasn't conched correctly. You'll also be able to drop words such as 'melting point', 'tempering' and 'nib winnowing' into conversations, thus further establishing your credentials as an expert.

Cacao trees are large things, standing some 20 metres high in the wild but slightly smaller – around three to eight metres – where farmed. They need a tropical climate to grow and are usually found around the equator, in places such as Venezuela, Côte d'Ivoire, Ghana, Indonesia and Brazil. They can be grown in greenhouses, but it's challenging and utterly impractical; at full maturity, a single tree still only produces enough beans for 1kg of chocolate. That would require an awful lot of very tall greenhouses.

BEAN AROUND THE WORLD

There are three main varieties of cacao bean: Criollo, Forastero and Trinitario.

Criollo translates as 'of local origin' and is the hardest variety to grow; it makes up about 5% of the world's cacao crop. In accordance with Murphy's Law, Criollo is also the best-quality bean, with a strong aroma and naturally lacking in bitterness. You'll find it in very high-quality chocolate, usually blended with other beans because otherwise it would be enormously expensive.

Forastero translates as 'foreigner' and is thought to have originated in the Amazon Basin. It makes up around 80% of the world's cacao crop and, as a result, is your common or garden cacao.

Making up most of the remaining 15% is Trinitario. The name contains its own aide mémoire in terms of origin, as it was developed on Trinidad after a hurricane wiped out the island's Criollo plantations. This bean is a hybrid of Criollo and Forastero. It's rich in fat and makes a very fine chocolate.

There are other regional varieties that will be considered in due course, but these are the main three you need to know about.

The beans grow in rugby-ball-shaped pods on the tree. Each pod takes about six months to ripen, and contains 30 to 40 seeds inside a lychee-like and edible pulp. When picked, the pods are broken open and the seeds laid out on banana leaves. They are then covered with more banana leaves and left in the heat to ferment for about a week. The fermentation reduces the bitterness and chocolate cannot be made unless the seeds have gone through this process.

Once fermented, the seeds can now be called beans. They must then be dried to reduce almost all of their moisture content. For those who like quoting figures (and what bluffer doesn't?), they lose up to 94% of moisture and about half their weight. This can be a challenge in rainy tropical climes, so it is often done in well-ventilated sheds. Some growers have been known to try to speed up the process by drying the beans with wood fires but this, unsurprisingly, can give the beans a smoky taste disliked by chocolate makers. On the plus side, a hint of smoke in the chocolate allows you to smack your lips, stare into the middle distance, and declare with appropriate concern that you suspect the grower was attempting to cut corners and dried these beans artificially. 'I'm afraid,' you will say with an air of mild distaste, 'that I detect a distinct residue of smoke.'

Once dried, the beans are then graded, bagged and shipped. Although a small amount of cacao is processed in its particular country of origin, the overwhelming majority is shipped around the world – though mostly to the Netherlands and the USA – to be processed.

After cleaning – to remove bits of twig, leaves, bark, insects, etc. – the beans are ready to be roasted. This is one of the stages that can greatly affect flavour further down the production line, both in terms of the length of time the roasting lasts (typically 10 to 35 minutes) and the temperature (typically 120–160°C).

The beans are then cooled and go through the next stage, which can be known as 'cracking' or 'fanning', to separate the shell from the kernel. The inside is what's known as the cocoa nib. The lighter outer husk/shell can be removed by applying a current of air, a process called 'winnowing' (or sometimes 'kibbling').

The nibs (plus sugar) then go for grinding in the mélangeur – thank you again, Mr Suchard – to form a smooth paste. At this point, the nibs contain around 53% cocoa butter.

The resulting paste can be called paste (but you probably guessed that), cocoa mass or liquor. This paste can, if required, be pressed – thank you, Mr van Houten – and separated into cocoa butter and cocoa powder.

MIXING IT UP

Mixing comes next, which helps define flavour and mouthfeel. If other ingredients – sugar, milk or vanilla, for example – are being added, they get mixed in. The chocolate is then refined further, either through a roll refiner or ball mill, which reduces the particle size of the cocoa mass and helps disperse the cocoa butter evenly. After mixing, the chocolate paste is smoother, but still some way from the finished product.

CONCHING

This brings us to the stage known as 'conching'. This has nothing to do with feral schoolboys creating their own dystopian society on a desert island, although the name does have a shell connection. The paddles used in this stage look like shells and the Spanish for 'shell' is *concha*.

It's basically a big mixer. The friction of the paddles creates heat, which melts the mixture, which helps with the main purpose of conching: reducing the particle size further and coating each particle with cocoa butter.

This stage also removes some of the less desirable qualities of the chocolate – it removes acetic acid, for example – and caramelises the sugars. It develops many of the flavours of the chocolate and, with more than 400 flavour compounds identified, it's both a vital part of the process and, arguably more importantly, your future chocolate expertise.

Even better than a comparison with an exclusive chocolate is the authoritative declaration that you suspect something went awry in the conching stage.

As will be discussed later, tasting chocolate – indeed, tasting anything – is all a matter of confidence. It's your palate, so it's your rules. If you declare a chocolate to be slightly grainy and a little burnt-tasting – or not as smooth and complex as that other chocolate you may or may not have tried – then it *is* slightly grainy and burnt-tasting. Even better than a comparison with an exclusive chocolate is the authoritative declaration that you suspect something went awry in the conching stage.

It used to be a case of the longer the conch, the better – four or five days was not unheard of in the old days. Modern technology has improved the efficiency of conching; eight hours is now a long time. The idea of 'the longer the better' is also something that will come under scrutiny later on, along with a few other chocolate myths.

And so now, you might think, the chocolate is ready to eat. Only it isn't. There are at least two stages to go before it becomes the finished article.

TEMPERING

What comes next is another useful part of the process for bluffing purposes. Tempering is what gives chocolate its appealing sheen and mouthfeel, which are also two more observations you will employ to establish your expertise.

The aim is to crystallise the cocoa butter and spread it evenly through the bar. The process – either by hand or machine – is laborious. The warm liquid chocolate is poured onto a marble slab, which helps it to cool. As you'll know from your experience of soup, the outer edges cool first. As it cools, the fat starts to crystallise. The cooler, starting-to-crystallise chocolate is then lifted back into the warmer, liquid middle. Other fat crystals will seed around these. As the process continues, they should be spread evenly throughout the mix. If they're not, that's when white smears appear, a sign that the fat is separating rather than crystallising. This is called 'blooming'.

BLOOMING

Insert your own 'blooming' appropriate joke at this point. It is also what happens when the finished chocolate product is allowed to get warm. If you've ever broken into a bar of 'bloomed' chocolate, you might have noticed that it crumbles rather than breaks with a satisfying snap. That's because the cocoa butter crystals have now pooled rather than remained evenly spread.

Once tempered, the chocolate can be kept stable in this liquid form or – finally – turned into bars. The liquid is poured into moulds, air bubbles removed – unless, one assumes, you're making a Wispa or an Aero – and left to cool.

A MATTER OF TASTE

And so, with the vocabulary and 'expertise' in place, it's time to put it all into practice.

Tasting, as mentioned previously, is a question of confidence. While it's easy to get steamrolled by tasting notes, labels, experts and other sources of information, approaching any food or drink item is all a question of confidence. It's your palate, your rules, and don't let anybody tell you otherwise.

It's what you think and whether you like it – and that means if you approach chocolate (or wine or whisky or anything) with a little knowledge, a little confidence and a sense of fun, you are about to enter a whole new world of bluffing.

You'll recall that chocolate contains more than 400 flavour compounds. Now you're about to get a rundown on the major ones but, if you'll excuse the *Charlie and the Chocolate Factory* reference, those flavour compounds are your golden ticket. There are no wrong answers. Whatever you say – particularly if accompanied by the recognised contemplative expression and a few of the moves listed below – is a perfectly acceptable answer. 'Hmm,' you can announce, with a contemplative chew and a frown of concentration, 'I'm getting a little smoke. Some red fruit. Maybe a little sparkle of eucalyptus, you know, like a New World Cabernet Sauvignon? And there's something else… blue cheese, perhaps? And there's a slight grassy hint…'

You can go the full Jilly Goolden if you want, and nobody can question you. Indeed, rather than question, they may well start following your lead and agreeing with you. So as well as learning the vocabulary, you may wish to practise your poker face in case you start sniggering.

The joy of chocolate tasting is that it involves all five senses, allowing you to be as theatrical or as subdued as you like.

THE TASTING SENSES

First, there's the **look.** If the chocolate is in its packaging, then the label – as you'll discover – can be your friend. Some labels give conching times, the origins of the beans, the percentage of cocoa solids used.

Once the chocolate is unwrapped, take a good look at it – front, back, sides, everywhere. Does it shine in that appealing glossy manner? Are there any obvious faults, such as blooming or air holes? (Or blooming air holes?) What colour is it? Learning your shades of brown – 'My, there's almost a hint of ochre', 'Goodness, it's positively teak-like' – is more ammunition for your perceived wisdom.

Now, it's time to **listen.** No, really. Snap off a square – or break the piece in two. Ask for silence as you bite into it – and see what noise it makes. A properly tempered bar of chocolate has a snap. Others may be slightly pliable before they break. Either way, you now know enough about tempering to say those wise words that will further establish your expertise.

You will taste it eventually but now it's time to **smell** the chocolate. Hold it gently in your fingers, let it warm between them. Inhale...then inhale again. There are numerous aromas that could hit you, from the fruity to the chemical, the earthy to the vegetable and all points in between. Again, there are no wrong answers – it's your nose, your rules – so feel free to be creative ('Yes, I'm getting damp, fresh hay on a spring morning, with a little mint and a hint of loganberry'), or stick to the more recognised aromas such as smoke, floral tones, nuts and toffee.

Now, to **touch.** Part of this – you'll be delighted to hear – is mouthfeel, so you do finally get to eat something. Just hold it there and let it melt and coat your tongue. The joy of this – aside from hopefully tasting something delicious – is that it will naturally give you that slightly pious look that works so perfectly in this scenario. While that's happening, consider how the chocolate is melting in terms of speed and how it feels – for example, is it even and soft, or slightly grainy? At this point, certain characteristics will start to come through. Many chocolates can be quite acidic; you'll recognise them because your mouth will produce more saliva instantly. Does the sensation linger? Are you left with that slightly puckered, dry feeling you get after drinking a particularly tannin-heavy red wine?

While doing this, the advanced bluffer may wish to rub a small piece of chocolate between the thumb and fingertips. A well-produced chocolate, with the cocoa butter evenly spread throughout, will melt into its constituent parts, the cocoa butter being absorbed into the skin, leaving a small amount of fat and powdery residue on your fingers. More mainstream chocolate will melt messily in your hand, due to the addition of vegetable fats rather than cocoa butter. It's a fun comparison that will also make you look smarter or, at least, provide an excuse as to why you've got a handful of molten Galaxy.

Conveniently, chocolate melts somewhere around mouth temperature.

Finally, the flavour. Yes, bluffing friends, it's time to **taste.** The reason the production process focuses on spreading the cocoa butter evenly throughout the bar is because the flavour notes are held in the fat. As the chocolate melts, the flavours are released. Conveniently, chocolate melts somewhere around mouth temperature.

So, consider the flavours you're noticing as you chew slowly. Also, does the flavour hit instantly and fade to nothing? Does it build gradually and change and linger on the tongue? Are there shifts in flavour or is it one note? Is it overpoweringly smoky so you can criticise the bean-drying process?

As mentioned above, there are certain broad flavours – floral, fruity, spicy, winey, etc. – that you might want to look for. The bolder among you, though, may wish to elaborate further.

Instead of floral, suggest which flower – rose, orange blossom, jasmine are good examples. Fruit can be red – berries, those winey flavours – or brighter and zesty – lemon, lime, grapefruit, etc. Rather than just 'nutty', specifying what sort of nutty – almond, hazel, brazil (you know the drill) – sounds rather more impressive. Instead of spicy, consider pepper – both white and black – or chilli, nutmeg, cumin or liquorice to name but a few. Similarly, you can go beyond smoky and suggest things like tobacco or wood smoke, even leather if you like, although that might lead to being asked how you know what leather tastes like, which is perhaps a whole new direction for the conversation to follow that you might not want to take part in.

READ THE LABEL

Earlier, the importance of the label was mentioned as playing an essential part in the tasting mix, not least because you can get a clue as to the possible ingredients and tailor-make your comments accordingly. The flavour of chocolate can be affected by all sorts of things, but key among these is the variety and origin of the beans used. While there's no guarantee that good beans will equate to good chocolate – a bad chocolate maker is still a bad chocolate maker even if they use the best possible ingredients – there are certain flavours associated with the type of beans used and where they've come from.

Like French wines, the notion of 'terroir' applies.* The soil and climate can affect the taste. For example, beans grown in places with greater rainfall can have a more earthy flavour, while beans from hot, dry regions tend towards acidic and brighter flavours. The chocolate maker – and the grower, and the fermentation process, etc. – will also have an effect but, assuming you're analysing a reportedly good bar, it's worth knowing some of the things to look for.

This works in two ways. If you've caught a glimpse of the label and it shows the variety of bean and/or source of origin, you can suggest the flavours associated with those. If you're feeling more confident, it's also a chance to show off and, if you cannot accurately identify the type of bean/country of origin, at least have a go. Even if you're wrong, there's enough overlap between regions and beans to justify why you made the suggestion you did. And it's impossible to stress just how useful those 400-plus flavour compounds are when it comes to such games.

*See *The Bluffer's Guide to Wine*.

KNOW YOUR BEANS

So it's very important that in any matter of taste you should know your beans, where they grow and what their distinctive flavours are.

You won't have forgotten that Criollo is the best of the three key cocoa beans and typically comes from Java, Madagascar and Venezuela. In terms of flavour, it's the most rounded of the three main beans but varies between regions. Criollo beans from Venezuela are more floral, while Madagascan beans give more acidity. Javan Criollo beans are well rounded – it's never a good idea to use the word 'chocolatey' but it's probably as good as any here – hence they're often used in milk chocolate as they give so much chocolate character.

The Trinitario bean hails mainly from Trinidad (obviously), Haiti, Jamaica, Venezuela (again) and Grenada. It's a milder flavour than the Criollo but is famed for its robust finish. If you've sampled a piece of chocolate with a lingering flavour, you can speculate – and not so wildly – that it features Trinitario beans. The bean's generally milder nature enables it to combine well with other beans. It typically has floral and fruit flavours/aromas, although the beans from Jamaica can have notes of rum and juniper. Rum notes, Jamaican origin; that should be easy enough to remember.

And there's no harm in repeating that Forastero is the most common bean in the chocolate-making world. It is full of typical chocolate character and low in bitterness. In terms of geographical origin, you'll need to remember the main producers: Côte d'Ivoire (tobacco, leather), São Tomé and Príncipe (it's okay, you won't be the first to have to look it up; they're islands off the west coast of Africa, and their beans have notes of red fruit and cinnamon) and Ghana (coffee flavours).

KNOW YOUR REGIONS, TOO

There are a lot of similarities among the main bean-producing regions, and with that enormous breadth of flavour compounds, it's all a bit of a bluffer's paradise. If you've speculated that there's a big hit of red fruit to what you're eating, thus you suspect it's Colombian, there's no shame in being told it's actually Jamaican or Bolivian or even Madagascan – particularly if you can respond with an 'Oh yes, I did wonder, I thought I detected a fleeting hint of orange…'

Bolivia As with many of the South American beans, red fruits are to the fore.

Colombia Red fruit. Again.

Côte d'Ivoire Tobacco and leather (careful) can be prominent, but beans produced here are regarded as well-rounded, making them both a very common ingredient in mass-produced chocolate and fine ones to mention in your tasting activities. 'Yes, I imagine it's been bulked out with Côte d'Ivoire Forastero beans,' is a statement you can make with utter conviction as, in many cases, it will be true.

Dominican Republic Big flavours, big aromas. Liquorice, molasses, deep caramel notes. Throw in phrases like 'sticky toffee pudding' and 'winter suppers'.

Ecuador Floral. You might also see the word 'Arriba' on labels. This is a variation on the Forastero bean. As fans of Speedy Gonzales might be aware, it means 'up' in Spanish and refers to beans grown upriver of the Guayas River Basin which, typically, are very floral. This will pay significant dividends in the unlikely event that you remember it.

Ghana Can you get away with saying 'chocolatey' again? Oh, alright then. As already noted, coffee flavours are typical, as are hints of tobacco. Mostly, though, Ghanaian beans are famed for a lack of bitterness and a robust chocolate flavour. It's another one you can mention in similar circumstances to Côte d'Ivoire beans. Or, indeed, mention both: 'There's Forastero here, I'd say, but I can't tell offhand if it's from Côte d'Ivoire or Ghana…'

Grenada Floral, woody, acidic, red fruit…there's a great variety to beans from Grenada, making it a good catch-all to suggest if analysing blind.

Indonesia Creamy, toffee and honey are all good words to use with Javan chocolate. It's often used in milk chocolate where such flavours and sweetness are desirable.

Jamaica Rum is possible (possibly because of spillage near the trees?), but woody notes are often evident, likewise a certain earthiness. Both of those can come from poor harvesting (another point you can make).

Madagascar As a contrast to the 'winter supper' notes of chocolate from the Dominican Republic, Madagascan beans are milder and more summery, with hints of tangerine-like fruits and slight acidity.

Mexico Happily, having started the whole thing (sort of) back in the day, Mexico is getting back into Criollo production. Keep an eye out if only because it's an excuse to recount all sorts of marvellous history.

São Tomé and Príncipe It's worth mentioning these tiny islands again, because few things are more satisfying than sending people running for their atlases (or, more likely, Google). Red fruits and cinnamon – plus vanilla – can be detected.

Trinidad Think Trinidad, think totally tropical: fresh citrus tastes, a little spice.

Venezuela The original home of Criollo and now home to two of the world's most sought-after strains of the bean, Chuao and Porcelana (although the latter can also be found in Mexico and Peru). Rather wonderfully for the bluffer's purposes, Chuao comes from the Chuao plantation: a relatively small 140 hectares of the Aragua valley located in Parque

Nacional Henri Pittier Rancho Grande, with a tiny colonial church where the beans are traditionally dried. Porcelana – which translates unsurprisingly as 'porcelain' – are paler than other varieties of bean and do indeed make a lighter bar. Venezuelan beans are prized for their qualities and can have a toasted bread hint to them. Don't confuse it with smoke (not a good chocolate flavour).

'Fair play to the Belgians for getting away with it for so long. It's bluffing on an international scale, and they deserve full credit for it.'

MYTH CONCEPTIONS

One of the most potent weapons in the bluffing arsenal is the ability to prove or disprove the myths, commonly held beliefs and misheld opinions surrounding your chosen subject. Happily, chocolate comes preloaded with lots of these. For something that's so easily accessible, there's a whole load of confusion out there that can be backed up or cleared up with just a little knowledge. In this chapter, you'll be provided with all the ammunition you need to discuss them, analyse them and then either define, disprove or support them. All, of course, to the amazement of your marvelling audience.

CHOCOLATE MAKER OR CHOCOLATIER?

There's a temptation to use the word 'chocolatier' when it comes to people in the industry. It's a great word: it's clearly French; it sounds terribly knowledgeable. However, it doesn't apply to everyone in the chocolate-making world.

So far, only the work of the chocolate maker has been considered in how chocolate is made, but there's more to it than that. A chocolate maker, you see, is a person – or a company – who buys and roasts cocoa beans and grinds them into chocolate.

A chocolatier is the next person in the industry, the one who takes chocolate that others have made and turns them into chocolates, i.e., the filled, nut-covered, dipped confections particularly popular on Valentine's Day, Mother's Day and, yes, well, every other kind of day including Christmas Day, Boxing Day and all points between Monday and Sunday.

There are many chocolatiers across the world. There are many in most major cities. There are far fewer chocolate makers because, as hopefully established, the process of making chocolate is damn near thankless; it's laborious, long and requires all sorts of specialised equipment. To be a chocolatier is still a challenging role – particularly to be a good one – but most don't make their own chocolate from the bean. They buy 'couverture' chocolate, melt it down and make their own creations.

Couverture translates as 'covering' and basically refers to the kind of chocolate that covers things. This typically has a higher percentage of cocoa butter (to give the finished chocolate item the desired sheen and snap), and comes in all sorts of forms, from drop-sized pieces to huge slabs. High-end bars – Valrhona, Mast Brothers, Amedei, etc. (*see* 'Bean to the Bar', page 77) – also qualify under this tag and are used to make other chocolates and desserts. (A company called Barry Callebaut is one of the largest producers of couverture in the world and although well known within the industry, you'd be forgiven for having never heard of it.)

BELGIAN CHOCOLATE IS THE BEST IN THE WORLD

You see them everywhere, from supermarkets to high-street chocolate chains and duty-free shops. The Belgian chocolate. It's fantastic, right? Er, no. It's not.

Well, to be fair, it's not bad, but it's not necessarily fantastic. There are some great Belgian chocolatiers and chocolate makers. However, the whole 'Belgian-chocolate-is-the-best-in-the-world' thing was just great marketing by those cunning Belgians in the 1980s.

As we've already established – well, as you can certainly deduce from the climate – no cacao is grown in Belgium. The Belgians haven't contributed greatly to the chocolate world in terms of production techniques or innovations. The phrase 'Belgian chocolate' simply refers to chocolates made with imported chocolate in Belgium. There's no distinct style, there's no distinct flavour, there's no guarantee of quality. It's all spin. Most other countries don't do it – have you ever heard of 'British chocolate'? – but hey, fair play to the Belgians for getting away with it for so long. It's bluffing on an international scale, and they deserve full credit for it.

70% CHOCOLATE IS ALWAYS THE BEST

Possibly the most common assertion from those who don't know better is that the higher the percentage of cocoa solids, the higher quality the chocolate.

They're wrong, as you'll delight in pointing out, courtesy of your new-found expertise. In fact, it's one of the most misleading things about chocolate, as 70% cocoa solids does not indicate good quality or good flavour. No percentage does. You will find great 70% chocolates on the shelves and truly terrible ones. The number alone doesn't mean anything. Not only could they be terrible beans to begin with, but the additional 30% could be made up of vegetable fats, artificial flavourings, sweeteners, chalk, bits of bird's nest, barbed wire…you get the drift. There are many other things that dictate the quality and the flavour, but the amount of cocoa solids isn't one of them.

Why has this misconception taken hold? Well, many recipes call for 70%, which certainly suggests that it's a guarantee of quality, and many of the most acclaimed bars in the world, such as Valrhona's, are typically 70% cocoa solids. So, when someone announces this as 'fact', enjoy the following few seconds of glory. Simply shake your head with a weary smile – it's not their fault that they're not as worldly-wise about chocolate as you – explain why they're incorrect, and suggest instead that they just buy the best dark chocolate that they can afford.

WHITE CHOCOLATE IS NOT CHOCOLATE

Technically, this is correct. White chocolate contains no cocoa solids and therefore is not chocolate. It is, though, made of cocoa butter – a minimum of 20% – plus milk powder – a minimum of 14% – and sugar. The rest can be made of things such as vegetable fat, and vanilla is often added for flavour.

Some chocolatiers – such as London's acclaimed Paul A Young – argue that, as long as it's made with all cocoa butter rather than vegetable fat, it should count as chocolate, which is also a rather nice corollary for any white chocolate pontificating you are able to do.

CHOCOLATE IS AN APHRODISIAC

We've already mentioned Montezuma's belief that chocolate helped him keep his reputed 500-plus wives happy (not to mention his 4,000 concubines) – and, one assumes, not just by giving them a box every now and again. Montezuma's reliance on chocolate resulted in the notion that the substance had aphrodisiac qualities among its other mystical – or otherwise – benefits.

The Mayan and Aztec belief that chocolate was so beneficial in so many ways extended to Spain, after Cortés introduced the court to the stuff. The Spanish then – and the rest of Europe – continued to associate chocolate with love. That, possibly, is why it's still now so strongly associated with romance and St Valentine's Day.

Chocolate, as we've already established, is a marvellously complex thing, and one that will continue to keep the scientists busy for a while. As mentioned previously, chocolate contains theobromine, a mild stimulant of the central nervous system. It also contains many other things, including phenylethylamine, and it helps to stimulate serotonin.

Now, you could get all scientific on these substances but, let's be honest, if you wanted to do that, you wouldn't have purchased this particular book. As soon as we start mentioning things like 'phenylethylamine is a natural monoamine alkaloid and a trace amine', you'll either run to Google in a panic, or close the covers, put the book on the shelf and find something less challenging and sleep-inducing. Mind you, it is a lovely phrase to drop into a conversation about chocolate if you can remember it.

What you really need to remember about phenyl-ethylamine and serotonin is that they are both mood-lifting agents. These substances are released by the brain naturally when we are happy. They are also released naturally by the brain when we are experiencing feelings of love and lust. The body reacts with a rise in blood pressure, an increase in heart rate and an improved mood. While it can't necessarily be proved that chocolate is an aphrodisiac, it certainly mimics the feelings of falling in love/lust and also gives an energy boost. It's thus understandable that chocolate has this reputation.

CHOCOLATE IS HIGH IN CAFFEINE

Chocolate contains many stimulants – to recap, as they're great words to learn, theobromine, phenylethylamine and serotonin. It also contains caffeine, but not in particularly significant amounts. As observed before, eating chocolate may perk you up, but it's probably not the caffeine: a typical 100g bar contains up to 30mg of caffeine. A regular-sized cup of coffee contains up to 100mg of caffeine.

CHOCOLATE IS BAD FOR YOU

Sadly, no amount of science, bluffed or otherwise, is going to justify a chocolate-heavy diet. While there are health benefits in chocolate, 14 Mars Bars a day will not help you work, rest or play, nor can you go to work on a Creme or Easter egg. A small daily amount of well-made, well-sourced dark chocolate (with a reasonable percentage of cocoa solids) can do you some good, though.

Sadly, no amount of science, bluffed or otherwise, is going to justify a chocolate-heavy diet.

Cocoa butter is high in stearic acid. It's a saturated fat but, conversely/wonderfully, unlike other saturated fats, research shows that stearic acid doesn't appear to raise cholesterol.

Chocolate is also a source of magnesium, copper, iron and zinc, plus polyphenols which have been linked to a decreased risk of heart disease.

With regard to teeth-rotting arguments, chocolate alone will not cause cavities. Cavities are caused by acid which is formed when bacteria in the mouth metabolise sugars and starches from ANY food; it's the acid that eats through the enamel. The problem is not getting busy enough with a toothbrush, rather than any particular foodstuff.

In better news, however, there's some evidence to suggest that the naturally occurring phosphates and protein in chocolate may actually protect tooth enamel. Also, the fat content of chocolate – thank you, cocoa butter – means that chocolate clears the mouth quicker than other sweet treats, thus reducing the length of contact with the teeth. Again, this isn't carte blanche to eat – or prescribe – 23 Creme Eggs a day. It is still all things in moderation…

Some people will argue that chocolate gives them a headache. You could argue that there's no scientific link between chocolate and migraines, quoting a 1997 study by the University of Pittsburgh, but, even with evidence on your side (well, a vague knowledge of a small bit of evidence), successful bluffing is also about knowing where to stop.

As for chocolate causing spots…it doesn't. Many dermatologists argue that diet as a whole plays no significant part in the development of acne. Unless, one assumes, you rub 17 melted Rolos into your pores.

The same goes for weight gain. All things are fine in moderation, and that includes chocolate. Another good reason to eat a well-made chocolate with a high percentage of cocoa solids is that it gives so much flavour in small quantities. Eat it slowly, savour, enjoy the health benefits and, hopefully, you won't crave larger amounts. That's the theory, anyway. The reality is very different but, sadly, despite extensive research, it doesn't hold true that if a little bit of chocolate does you good, then a whole lot of chocolate must be even better for you.

CHOCOL-ART

As the experienced bluffer will be very aware, few things suggest knowledge, experience and education like a well-timed quote or *bon mot*. Happily, chocolate has inspired many literary greats – from George Bernard Shaw to Charles M Schulz – to discuss chocolate. Whole books have been written on the subject. Films have been made about it. And reading, watching and studying them will take more time than you have.

Some of the chocolate-themed or chocolate-referencing artistic works are worth a look when you have a moment. Surely there are few out there who don't recall *Charlie and the Chocolate Factory* – the (still) marvellous book, not the 1971 musical film based on it or the Tim Burton 'reimagining'. However, in the following pages, you will be apprised of the basic information you need to know without ever having to suffer Johnny Depp's underwhelming performance or appalling strained rhymes along the lines of 'oompa loompa doopity da, if you're not spoiled then you will go far.' Yes. Exactly.

CHARLIE AND THE CHOCOLATE FACTORY

Indeed, Roald Dahl is a good place to start. *Charlie and the Chocolate Factory* – the book, this can't be stressed enough – is a celebration of all things sweet, including good behaviour in children. If you haven't read it, then if you expect to become an accomplished chocolate bluffer you will need at the very least to know the plot.

The main character is Charlie Bucket. Charlie, his parents and his four grandparents – Mr Bucket's parents, Grandpa Joe and Grandma Josephine, and Mrs Bucket's parents, Grandpa George and Grandma Georgina – are very poor and live in 'a small wooden house on the edge of a great town'.

Charlie loves chocolate but only gets one bar a year, on his birthday. To make it worse, the Buckets live in sight and smell of the world's most famous – and secretive – chocolate factory, Wonka's Factory, owned by Mr Willy Wonka, 'the greatest inventor and maker of chocolates that there has ever been'.

One day, Wonka announces a competition. Five golden tickets will be hidden in bars of his chocolate, and the finders will be allowed to see inside the factory. Four tickets are found quickly. The first finder is Augustus Gloop, a fat boy who eats as a hobby. The second is found for Veruca Salt, a spoiled brat whose father bought thousands of bars to help her get one of the prized tickets. The third goes to the obnoxious, gum-chewing Violet Beauregarde, and the fourth is found by TV addict Mike Teavee. The fifth – thanks to a found 50-pence piece that he spends on two bars of

Wonka's Whipple-Scrumptious Fudgemallow Delight – goes to Charlie, so he and Grandpa Joe join the tour.

During the tour, the visitors discover the secret of Wonka's mystery employees – Oompa Loompas, direct from Loompaland – and the first four children are undone by their particular flaws. The greedy Gloop drinks from Wonka's chocolate river – 'No other factory in the world mixes its chocolate by waterfall! But it's the only way to do it properly!' He then tumbles in and is sucked up a pipe. Beauregarde ignores advice and falls foul of an experimental three-course meal in a stick of gum that turns her into a blueberry. Salt decides she wants one of the squirrels that Wonka uses to sort nuts but the squirrels test her for flaws – by rapping her on her head – and discard her down the chute for bad nuts. Teavee hijacks an experiment, transmits himself across the room by TV, and ends up an inch tall. As the only survivor, and because at least in children's fiction the nice guy wins, Charlie is awarded the factory by Willy Wonka.

That's the proper story. The first film version cast Gene Wilder as Willy Wonka (wrong, because as every chocolate lover knows, Willy Wonka is tiny, dark-haired and has a beard), added songs, and ignored pretty much everything Roald Dahl had done. Although Dahl wrote the original screenplay, director Mel Stuart brought in (the uncredited) David Seltzer to rewrite it. There was so little of Dahl's vision left – they even make Charlie badly behaved, which completely misses the point – that the author disowned the film and then refused to sell the film rights to the sequel, *Charlie and the Great Glass Elevator*.

Tim Burton's remake is perhaps even worse, which is a remarkable achievement. While more faithful to Dahl's story, Johnny Depp is woefully miscast (seriously, a pointy beard, is it too much to ask?) and is apparently channelling Michael Jackson in his pale-faced, effeminate and high-pitched performance. Burton also attempts to explain Wonka's love of sweets by inventing an evil dentist father played by Christopher Lee, adding a whole new level of wrongness to the adaptation.

CHOCOLAT

Joanne Harris fares better with a more faithful film adaptation of her book *Chocolat*. Interestingly, and a point you can drop in with absolute confidence, is that this tale of a woman and her daughter who open a chocolate shop in a small French village that greatly affects the locals' behaviour – particularly romantically – has parallels with an earlier novel/film, *Like Water For Chocolate*, a story that is actually more about food generally than chocolate. But, and here's the point, it also touches on some of the mood-enhancing, possible aphrodisiac qualities of chocolate.

The chocolatier, Vianne (played in the film by Juliette Binoche), arrives in a small village that's governed by the strict Comte de Reynaud (Alfred Molina). Much to his annoyance, Vianne opens her new tempting chocolate shop during Lent and the Comte attempts to prevent the villagers trying her delicious wares. Those who do discover that Vianne has a gift for prescribing their perfect chocolate confection, reawakening passions that had died, solving family problems (for her landlady played by Judi Dench), and giving the bar owner's wife Josephine Muscat (Lena Olin) the confidence to leave her violent, drunk husband. Eventually, the temptations of the bean prove too much for Reynaud, who finally tries the chocolate accidentally after breaking into the shop to destroy the window display. As a result, he becomes more tolerant and everybody's life is better, and it's all thanks to chocolate. And Johnny Depp plays a wandering, guitar-playing Irish gypsy called Roux who Vianne falls for and who is possibly loathed even more than she is by her fellow villagers. Irritatingly, in this film he actually wears the beard he should have worn in *Charlie and the Chocolate Factory.*

So, there you go. Chocolate's a mood enhancer. Everyone's life is improved. You can now pad that out with other choice comments – 'Yes, the chemistry between Depp and Binoche is remarkable,' or 'I like the scene when Roux is talking to the girl's imaginary kangaroo friend; that's very touching' – or draw parallels to *Like Water For Chocolate*, without ever having to see the films or read the books.

LIKE WATER FOR CHOCOLATE

This story treads very similar ground, but be careful, as there is a greater depth to the tale. It was the first novel by Mexican author Laura Esquivel. In Spanish, the title is *Como Agua Para Chocolate*, which you are recommended to use, particularly if anybody else mentions the English title first. Yes, it's an obvious and old trick, but a good one.

The story follows Tita de la Garza, the youngest daughter of three, living near the border between Mexico and the USA. According to tradition, the youngest daughter must remain unmarried and take care of her mother until the mother dies. Tita is in love with neighbour Pedro who asks for her hand in marriage, but her mother is unwavering.

Tita is an excellent cook, and she finds that her emotions pass into the food she prepares, leaving those that eat it elated, annoyed, lusty, etc., depending on Tita's feelings at the time. The book is split into 12 chapters, one per month, and each starts with a traditional Mexican recipe.

It's a marvellously complex tale, meaning that those who have read it or seen the excellent film adaptation (directed by Alfonso Arau) – both of which came out over 20 years ago – probably won't remember much about it. The scant details, then: Pedro marries Tita's sister to be closer to Tita. The sister conveniently dies. The mother is also dead by this point. Pedro proposes to Tita. She accepts. They have sex. There's a fire. They die. The only thing that survives is her book of recipes. The end.

The key things to remember here are the presence of the recipes, the emotions getting passed on via food and that the title is a phrase that means that one is angry. We've mentioned earlier that the original chocolate drink was made with water rather than milk. The metaphor is for the near boiling water that could be used to make it, hence 'so angry they're like water for chocolate' – or, better, *como agua para chocolate*.

IMPORTANT CHOCOLATE QUOTES

So, those are some of the key chocolate literature and film references for you, should the subjects or opportunity arise. Should time not permit for a full discussion on books you haven't read or films you haven't seen, here are some fine quotes to memorise, together, where applicable, with a little useful background (as being specific can always add conviction). And all are better than that inevitable Forrest Gump line, so you would be advised to ignore that and let someone else quote it.

What use are cartridges in battle? I always carry chocolate instead.

George Bernard Shaw, *Arms and the Man*

The line is spoken by Captain Bluntschli, a Swiss mercenary fighting in the Serbo-Bulgarian War, to Raina Petkoff, a young Bulgarian woman engaged to another. The two ultimately end up together. She also refers to Bluntschli as 'My chocolate-cream soldier', which inspired the name of *The Chocolate Soldier*, the 1908 operetta written by Oscar Straus and based on Shaw's play.

Venice is like eating an entire box of chocolate liqueurs in one go.

Truman Capote

All you need is love. But a little chocolate now and then doesn't hurt.

Charles M Schulz, the creator of Peanuts

The wisdom of *Charlie Brown* cartoons is rarely misplaced.

> *There is nothing better than a friend, unless it is a friend with chocolate.*
>
> Linda Grayson, children's author

Rather marvellously – particularly when someone you're attempting to trump quotes the above and *The Pickwick Papers* – this quote is often attributed to Charles Dickens. It's not Dickens, it's Grayson. She has a website called The Printwick Papers which, thanks to the joys of idiots on the internet, was misread as The Pickwick Papers. A chocolate quote AND the chance to lance an urban legend is the stuff bluffing dreams are made of.

> *'Without pain, how could we know joy?' This is an old argument in the field of thinking about suffering and its stupidity and lack of sophistication could be plumbed for centuries but suffice it to say that the existence of broccoli does not, in any way, affect the taste of chocolate.*
>
> John Green, *The Fault in Our Stars*

The book is a tale about a cancer patient called Hazel and a man she meets at a support group. The quote has the benefit that the full thing suggests your reading is wide and all-inclusive, while the pay-off line, from 'the existence of broccoli...', is a great line that can shift a discussion on the good and bad of life into a discussion on your new area of expertise.

'Can I come back and see you sometime?'
'Long as you bring me some chocolate,' Gramma said,
*   and smiled. 'I'm partial to chocolate.'*
'Gramma, you're diabetic.'
'I'm old, girl. Gonna die of something. Might as well
*   be chocolate.'*
Rachel Caine, *The Dead Girls' Dance*

Like the previous quote, the final line of this stands alone in certain situations, such as the inevitable argument that chocolate isn't good for you. The book it comes from is actually a part of a teenage series on vampires. No, not that one. Another one.

Your hand and your mouth agreed many years ago that,
as far as chocolate is concerned, there is no need to involve
your brain.

Dave Barry, American humorist

Chocolate says 'I'm sorry' so much better than words.
Rachel Vincent, *My Soul to Save*

This is from yet another teenage series of books with a vaguely occult theme. In this instance it's a series called *Soul Screamers* about a girl who can kill with her voice. Unless you have a teenage daughter, you may wish to choose between the relevant quotes in case someone begins to question your reading tastes.

Anything is good if it's made of chocolate.

Jo Brand, British comedian

Happiness. Simple as a glass of chocolate or tortuous as the heart. Bitter. Sweet. Alive.

Joanne Harris, *Chocolat*

A useful one to have prepped should your *Chocolat* credentials need an extra boost.

What you see before you, my friend, is the result of a lifetime of chocolate.

Katharine Hepburn

Another commonly used quote and another that you can raise questions about should someone beat you to the punch. Film producer John Philip Dayton contacted an online quote resource to question the use of 'my friend'. His argument? 'She might have said it, but without the "my friend". This is a phrase I have never, ever, heard her utter, and it would be highly uncharacteristic of her to do so. As far as the chocolate part goes, that, indeed is Kate.'

As with most fine things, chocolate has its season. There is a simple memory aid that you can use to determine whether it is the correct time to order chocolate dishes: any month whose name contains the letter A, E, or U is the proper time for chocolate.

Sandra Boynton, author,
Chocolate: The Consuming Passion

Boynton is a humorist, children's author (those with young children may recognise her name from *Hippos Go*

Berserk!) – and writer of *Chocolate: The Consuming Passion*, a whimsical look at all things cocoa. The reason the author wrote the book is also highly quotable: '14 out of 10 people like chocolate.'

> *The greatest tragedies were written by the Greeks and Shakespeare…neither knew chocolate.*
>
> Sandra Boynton

> *Always serve too much hot fudge sauce on hot fudge sundaes. It makes people overjoyed, and puts them in your debt.*
>
> Judith Olney, food and cookery writer

Olney writes about and teaches cookery. She's also a former restaurant critic and food editor at the *Washington Times*.

> *The 12-step chocolate program: NEVER BE MORE THAN 12 STEPS AWAY FROM CHOCOLATE!*
>
> Terry Moore, American comic book author

> *Every now and then, I'll run into someone who claims not to like chocolate, and while we live in a country where everyone has the right to eat what they want, I want to say for the record that I don't trust these people, that I think something is wrong with them, and that they're probably – and this must be said – total duds in bed.*
>
> Steve Almond, *Candyfreak: A Journey Through the Chocolate Underbelly of America.*

The appropriately named Almond is a teacher-turned-writer with a candy obsession, who toured the USA to find regional treats and charted his tour in this book.

> *Flowers wilt, jewellery tarnishes and candles burn out…but chocolate doesn't hang around long enough to get old.*
>
> Sr Cocoa Loco

Unsurprisingly, Sr Cocoa Loco isn't a real name. It's a pseudonym used by one Daniel Worona, who has compiled a vast collection of food-related jokes and humour for what he calls the Laugh It Off Diet, based around the theory that several good laughs a day help you burn calories; '100 laughs a day is equal to 10 minutes of exercise,' he reasons. The exercise equivalent of a few hard-won smiles isn't documented and, frankly, would be more appropriate (if you're British).

> *Chocolate symbolises, as does no other food, luxury, comfort, sensuality, gratification and love.*
>
> Karl Petzke

Petzke is a photographer and author of *Chocolate: A Sweet Indulgence*, a glossy, slightly lascivious celebration of chocolate. He does nail the substance with that line, though, and has the sort of name that people will think they should have heard of. Perfect quoting material, then.

Chocolate is like my best friend and the most intense pleasure at the same time, perhaps not the most intense, but the most regular and reliable one.

Chloe Doutre-Roussel,
author, *The Chocolate Connoisseur*

Caramels are only a fad. Chocolate is a permanent thing.
Milton Snavely Hershey

Hershey (1857–1945) was a confectioner, philanthropist and founder of the Hershey Chocolate Company, which now produces a dull, brown, wax-like substance masquerading as chocolate.

When we don't have the words chocolate can speak volumes.
Joan Bauer, American author and journalist

Oh, divine chocolate!
They grind thee kneeling,
Beat thee with hands praying,
And drink thee with eyes to heaven.

Marco Antonio Orellana (1731–1813),
Spanish writer, getting lyrical on the subject

If some confectioners were willing
To let the shape announce the filling,
We'd encounter fewer assorted chocs,
Bitten into and returned to the box.

Ogden Nash, American poet and writer,
taking a slightly less reverential approach

You know, they've got these chocolate assortments, and you like some but you don't like others? And you eat all the ones you like, and the only ones left are the ones you don't like as much? I always think about that when something painful comes up. Now I just have to polish these off, and everything'll be OK. Life is a box of chocolates. I suppose you could call it a philosophy.

Haruki Murakami, *Norwegian Wood*

Japanese author Murakami provides the final word to expose anyone whose contribution to this conversation involves Tom Hanks and a Southern US accent.

MATCHMAKERS

As has been (hopefully) established already, chocolate is potentially bursting with flavours. Never forget that well-made, well-sourced chocolate can contain more than 400 flavour profiles, which is how it can be turned so successfully into so many unusually flavoured things.

Knowing some of these odd combinations is a highly efficient way of implying your chocolate expertise. Similarly, being able to match a chocolate to a drink – be it tea, coffee, beer, wine or a spirit – can suggest a greater depth of knowledge than you actually possess.

You could spend hours matching different chocolates to different drinks or unusual ingredients. You could roll your sleeves up, get your hands dirty and actually make something unusual and chocolatey. But in the time it's going to take you to bake, for example, a chocolate and beetroot cake, you could have read this chapter twice, taken notes and enjoyed a little nap. Admittedly, that way you don't then have a slice of deliciously moist cake to enjoy – the sweet earthiness of beetroot works extremely well with chocolate – but the choice is yours. For many of you, the knowledge that chocolate and beetroot work well together will be sufficient. For those people, we'd like to point out that chocolate and courgette also make a fine cake. And if anyone ever guffaws at the suggestion – 'vegetables in dessert?' – ask them how many times they've eaten carrot cake and what they think might give that its name.

So, in the coming pages, prepare yourself for a look at some of the odd combinations of chocolate and food and drink that work well, including, where possible, an explanation of why; after all, conviction and a little evidence go a long way in bluffing.

CHOCOLATE AND CHEESE

Let's start bold; after all, it's the extremes, the unexpected combinations, that are going to best illustrate your perceived expertise. Chocolate and wine, chocolate and whisky, chocolate and fruit, etc., are all very well – and can actually be more problematic than you'd think – but they're obvious pairings. Many – if not all – of your audience will have tried these in some way, shape or form. No, in order to impress, you've got to go hard or go home, hence the seemingly odd combination of chocolate and cheese.

Be warned: some of your audience may already have tried this. Several chocolatiers have produced cheese-based products, such as port and Stilton truffles. English chocolatier and pâtissier Paul A Young also has a spring chocolate of goats' cheese and rosemary. Even the mainstream has got involved, thanks to that recent

Philadelphia/Cadbury's pairing which you'll need to remember. Happily, though, for our purposes, chocolate and cheese still sounds like the work of mad scientists – the kind of combination that would make even Heston Blumenthal say, 'Easy chaps, I think we might have gone too far…'

A fun fact to point out – probably best to improvise a gentle laugh or a wry smile – is that, actually, all of your audience members are likely to have experienced the chocolate/cheese combination. When they deny it, suggest – again employing that wry smile – that they just add the word 'cake' to those two words because, hey, who hasn't tried chocolate cheesecake? Aside from the lactose intolerant, of course. Or the diabetics. But let's not digress. Somehow, people who'd never think of eating, say, a square of single-origin 70% Venezuelan with a piece of mature Cheddar will almost certainly have wolfed a slice of something that's basically a mash-up of cream cheese, chocolate and digestive biscuits.

It's then time to push the envelope a little more and expand on the theory. You'll recall how so many chocolate varieties have strong notes of red fruit or a crisp acid bite. Many chutneys are similarly fruity and/or acidic thanks to the addition of vinegar. You'd happily eat the latter, so why not a little chocolate instead? Likewise, much dark chocolate contains tannins, similar to a red wine. You'd certainly enjoy that aforementioned mature Cheddar while supping a glass of red so, actually, is an accompaniment of chocolate really such a quantum leap? (Which is actually a very small thing but sounds like a very big thing – see *The Bluffer's Guide to the Quantum Universe*.)

The rules of wine matching with cheese can generally be applied here. There are many exceptions – while those 400-plus flavour profiles often work in your favour, you're still pairing the strongly flavoured with the similarly strongly flavoured – but the basic rules are a good place to start. You don't drink something heavy and tannic with a rich and creamy cheese because a meaty Cabernet Sauvignon and a slab of Brie is a mouth-furring mistake you should only make once. Fruity works. Creamy works; there's a bit of a clue in the cheese's texture, frankly. Matching like for like is generally a good rule of thumb. Experimenting is fun, yes, but it's also potentially disgusting. Just remember – and declare with some authority – that cheese is basically a milk storage system, invented to prolong the life of all the good stuff that came out of cows. Chocolate, to a lesser extent, is the same. Some good-quality chocolate, with a little acid and fruit, thus works well with a creamy cheese. Stilton, for example, is a great one to match, as its flavour profile has many similarities to chocolate. Creamy, earthy, that tang of the blue, perhaps some nuttiness…you can see where this is going.

CHOCOLATE AND SAVOURY

Chocolate can be used in many savoury recipes. The obvious one that springs to mind – or at least will from this point on – is the Mexican 'mole' sauce. Always pronounce it 'mole-lay'. Happily, a lot of people assume that it's a rich, thick, chocolate-heavy sauce, probably because they've had lazy versions in terrible Tex-Mex places. The real mole – which for the purposes of this book you must be well acquainted with (even if only vicariously through these pages) – is so much more than that, which you can gleefully point out to your audience. There are several variations of mole, in terms of colour, ingredients, region, etc., but it's generally assumed that you mean *mole poblano* which features a very small amount of chocolate among its 20 to 30 ingredients (depending on which of several hundred recipes you use). By the end of preparation, the sauce doesn't taste particularly of chocolate; it melts and just gives depth of flavour and a really silky texture.

> Experimenting with chocolate and cheese is fun, yes, but it's also potentially disgusting.

For the same reasons, a little grated chocolate in a meat stew or a chilli also works surprisingly well. Not that it surprises you, of course, because you are now a worldly-wise, chocolate genius. You can also illustrate the joys of meat and chocolate further by casually mentioning that the Gaucho chain of steak restaurants offer a novel *petit four*: a chocolate made with a beef stock reduction.

You can further opine on chocolate's innate ability to go well with so many things by discussing the rise in popularity of salt as an ingredient, particularly the 'cult' of the salted caramel chocolate.

Sea-salted caramel originated in Brittany – an area that has access to a lot of butter and sea salt so, necessity being the mother of invention, they tend to use it wherever they can. Inspired by the combination, Pierre Hermé, the celebrated Parisian pastry chef, produced a salted caramel macaron. In 2003, London's Artisan du Chocolat created a liquid salted caramel chocolate for Gordon Ramsay's restaurant. Other chocolatiers followed. Restaurants followed. Even Starbucks followed with a salted caramel-flavoured hot chocolate, while Marks & Spencer launched a sea-salted caramel sauce. Going beyond that, Lindt now has a successful dark chocolate variety, A Touch of Sea Salt, and Green & Black's produces a sea-salt milk chocolate bar. In less than a decade, salted chocolate/caramel/all of the above went from bold combination to novelty cult item and onwards to, in a sense, culinary world domination.

CHOCOLATE AND WINE

If cheese's complex flavours prove a good match, the same has to apply to wine. Yes, it's obvious, but if others discuss it, you need to be able to hold your own.

The two substances seem to be natural companions, as the tasting process for each is similar – from analysing the appearance, to gently testing the aroma, to finally savouring the flavours and mouthfeel. If testing both together, you might take a sip of wine, followed by a tiny piece of chocolate and then, as the chocolate begins to melt, a second sip. And all accompanied, somewhat inevitably, by that middle-distance stare and slight frown you are by now perfecting. Slurps and lip smacking are also permitted, but do practise in private first as dribbling and spraying your audience with saliva can seriously undermine your air of authority.

A lot of wine and a lot of chocolate will share similar flavours. Things you should comment on are the acidity, the fruit, the tannins and the other flavours you notice. And remember: it's your palate, your nostrils – and whose rules? Yes, quite right, your rules. If you're feeling confident, let them have it: 'Pine trees. Beetroot. A hint of floor polish. There's an underlying haggis note. Roasted meats. Raisins. Key limes…'

If you're not confident enough to have fun with the analysis stage – or just want to illustrate your points and knowledge – you can always jump straight to the more successful pairings. For a dark chocolate, with tannin and acidity, try something like a Zinfandel or a tawny port. For milk chocolate – which typically has less acidity and more sweetness – soft, sweet wines like Muscatel are a safe bet. Riesling and Sauvignon Blanc can be good. Dessert wines are also often a safe option. Do bear in mind that you might not like these combinations but that others might – and vice versa.

CHOCOLATE AND OTHER DRINKS

Despite chocolate's broad range of flavours, gin and vodka are something of a struggle to match with it, mostly due to their dryness and, certainly in straight, non-infused vodka's case, its frequent lack of any distinct flavour. Rum is a good bet – bring on the Jamaican chocolate – and whisky is safer still. Whisky typically contains vanilla and caramel notes because of the bourbon casks often used for maturation, or has sweeter raisin notes if finished in a sherry cask. The label should specify this, and that makes it a gift for the experienced – or otherwise – chocolate expert. Many, particularly the Islay whiskies, have a saltiness to them which sits very well alongside salted chocolates and salted chocolate caramels. A successful pairing of those and the brief history of salted caramel should put you in very good stead. Coffee is also a relatively safe bet to pair with chocolate.

CHOCOLATE AND OTHER FLAVOURS

Where do you start? More to the point, where do you finish? Lindt now offers a bar with wasabi (Japanese horseradish) in national supermarkets, along with a surprisingly palatable chilli chocolate bar. Paul A Young's bestselling chocolate is flavoured with Marmite (it's surprisingly good) – and then Marmite swiftly stepped in and did its own 'Very Peculiar' 100g bar combining its distinctive yeast spread with 98% milk chocolate and 2% Marmite flavouring (including onion and garlic powder). American chocolatier Vosges offers an Applewood Smoked Bacon bar. At The Fat Duck restaurant, Heston Blumenthal has served an Artisan du Chocolat tobacco chocolate as a *petit four* – he's also been known to serve a cauliflower risotto with a chocolate jelly. Swiss chocolate maker Akessons grows beans and pepper and combines the two in their bars. And nearly everybody has experimented with chilli at one time or another – sometimes to memorable effect.

MAKE IT AND BAKE IT

Forgive us for mentioning this again but it is bluffing gold: chocolate has over 400 recognisable flavour profiles making it a dream for straightforward AND more creative pairing.

But what about baking? Thanks to *that* TV programme, baking has suddenly become fashionable and aspirational. Oneupmanship used to be about your house, your car, your job, your possessions – now it can include the age of your sourdough starter, the smoothness of your buttercream, your ability with a palate knife, and your defiant lack of a soggy bottom.

Chocolate – in all its myriad forms – can be a surprising challenge when it comes to baking. Get it right, and you'll be given a parade and the freedom of the city and before you know it you'll be herding sheep over Tower Bridge… or maybe not. But other bakers will give you one of *those* nods, those looks of absolute respect, because they know the challenge of packing chocolate flavour into cakes and such like. Most people won't, of course, but then under-appreciation is the perfect opportunity to bluff, a chance to hold court and share your *bon mots*, your little snippets of wisdom. We've all experienced those cakes and biscuits and brownies that glint with chocolate-y promise, that ooze a centre of pure molten chocolate, that seem stuffed to breaking point with gorgeous chips of joy that then taste of, well . . . nothing much except sweetness and which prove to be less chocolate, more just brown. Ah, you can declare, what a pity. If only they'd used cocoa instead of hot chocolate / a higher percentage bar / whisked things more thoroughly...

Baking is often described as the most scientific of the domestic cookery processes, and so you must describe it in the same way. Watching the likes of Mary Berry measure flour and butter by eye is not a trick to be undertaken by the rank amateur. Behind that casual stir is a deep understanding of the balance between the various ingredients – flour, eggs, milk, water, sugar, flavourings, raising agent, etc., – and elements – size, temperature, length of mixing etc., all of which can change the taste and texture of the resulting treat.

In the current absence of a *Bluffer's Guide to Baking*, here then are a few tips for chocolate use and general baking, for you to memorise and, in due course, pass off as supreme culinary wisdom.

As mentioned above, baking – and this cannot be stressed enough – is a science. As such, it's very easy to derail the end result: incorrectly graded scales, incorrectly calibrated measuring spoons and cups, incorrectly marked oven dials – all can cause problems in the end result – and all should be celebrated as rich in bluffing potential.

If you want to illustrate baking in layman's terms – and you do, because it makes you sound more knowledgeable – bear in mind the following. Some ingredients provide structure. Others are there for softness. Some are there for flavour. And some – chocolate for example – serve more than one purpose.

Chocolate, along with flour and egg white, can bring structure. You can, if you wish, liken these to concrete and steel, the load-bearing elements of the equation. The softness comes from the tenderising ingredients such as sugar, fat and egg yolks. Chocolate, while containing fat and sugar, adds flavour but also adds strength.

As a simple rule of thumb, use the best quality chocolate you can find. That's not to say you should cheerfully throw your carefully sourced, enormously expensive bar of single estate, artisan chocolate into the bowl but inferior chocolate will result in inferior cakes, brownies or cookies.

Brownies, in particular, are the absolute sum of their parts. The ingredients list is typically short – eggs, butter, flour, sugar, chocolate, cocoa – meaning each element is key in terms of texture, flavour and appearance. Upping the amount of cocoa powder, for example, will add flavour but also leave you with a drier texture: if your intention was to create the perfect chocolate fudge brownie, you're going to be disappointed. Similarly, if you use baking chocolate or chocolate chips, these often contain other ingredients – stabilisers, vanilla flavourings, sugar – which will change the texture and flavour. Using chocolate you can eat straight from the bar is a very good place to start – and an easy rule to remember for bluffing purposes.

Another key thing to remember here – as mentioned in earlier observations about 70% chocolate – is the matter of what constitutes the remaining 30%. If it's sugar, quelle surprise! It will affect the overall sweetness of your recipe. You should also bear in mind that cocoa powder and hot chocolate are not interchangeable: the former is unsweetened, the latter will contain sugar in some form. The fat content is also important to note. Accordingly, using milk chocolate in much baking will result in a confection that's more sugar than flavour, or rather more oily than intended.

The way your chocolate is added is also important. If it's for texture – chips in cookies, for example – break your chocolate into small pieces and add them as late as possible: this will give them less time to sink (another common problem which can be rectified by applying your new-found wisdom – and one that also applies to fruit). Dusting chocolate (and fruit) with flour will also slow the sinking process.

If it's for flavour, you will want it melted. The microwave can be useful here but it is very easy to overcook/burn. The long established, professionally acceptable method is the *bain marie*: place your chocolate in a bowl, then place that bowl in/over a hot water bath: this melts the chocolate slowly and, as a result, avoids potential graininess and overcooking.

Another key point to remember is that the size of the chocolate pieces will change the melting process. Small, even pieces melt evenly. Big uneven chunks of chocolate take longer, increasing the chance of burning.

It's also important when baking – remember, this

is science after all – that ingredients are added in the correct order, so don't be tempted to experiment. Don't skip the steps outlined in your recipe, and follow the rules. Chocolate is a capricious mistress.

The delicate balance of ingredients can even be affected by the lack of bowl scrape. Whatever is left in the bowl could be an essential part of the equation. Also, the way in which the ingredients have been mixed plays a vital part. That need for even distribution is very important: pockets of flour, sugar or, particularly, raising agent will affect flavour, texture and even shape.

Even using the wrong sugar can also change the texture. If the recipe calls for caster sugar, granulated sugar may not be a suitable alternative, and could result in grittier-than-desired results.

While nobody wants a disappointing cake, being armed with several convincing reasons for the lack of flavour or underwhelming texture is a sensible precaution. You don't even have to be right: it's simply enough to justify the aspersions you're casting.

And finally, even if the cake in front of you is utter perfection, you can still add your bluffer's two pennyworth. Declare it delicious but speculate how much better it could be with a pinch of salt because, salt is one of chocolate's best friends and, in the manner of the ubiquitous salted caramel, brings out more of its inherent sweetness and flavours.

ß

What finer way to trump another guest's expensive gift of handmade chocolates than to compare it to an even more obscure product from the other side of the world?

BEAN TO THE BAR

As already defined, the chocolate maker is the person – or manufacturing business – that takes the processed cocoa beans and turns them into chocolate. Indeed, many brag about their 'bean-to-bar' credentials and, to be fair, given the alchemy involved in making a decent bar of chocolate, we should probably allow them a little bravado.

The chocolate produced by some of these people is becoming more readily available around the world, both in bar form and via chocolatiers using the chocolate makers' products in their own creations. The chocolatiers will be introduced shortly but, for now, it's enough to focus on some of these makers, if only so you can adopt a tone of gravitas and use phrases like 'artisan micro-batch production'. Remember that one.

There are many people around the world making chocolate and the numbers are going up all the time. For the purposes of this section, it's enough to focus on some of the best the UK has to offer and a few choice places from around the world. By the time you're finished, you'll be able to make it sound like you've helped them sort the beans, gauged the roast, watched them winnow, corrected their tempering process and stuck the labels on.

MAST BROTHERS

Brooklyn is one of those places that is a Mecca to the young artisan food producer, so it was perhaps inevitable that someone would start making chocolate there. Two people, in fact: brothers Rick and Michael Mast. Rick used to be a chef at chic New York places such as Soho House and the Gramercy Tavern. Michael was in the finance side of the film industry. They both have impressive creative-type beards. Their shop/factory features a lot of bare brick and wood – you can imagine the artisan look – and their wrappers are particularly distinctive, with some reminiscent of the ornate papers you find on the inside covers of old hardback books, and others that look like old architect's/draughtsman's drawings.

They source beans from Venezuela, Madagascar and the Dominican Republic. They also change their range on a regular basis, adding different flavours and ingredients, such as almonds and sea salt, chilli pepper, and coffee from New York roasters Stumptown. The plain Madagascar bar is regarded by many as a masterpiece. It's 72% cocoa solids, and most suggest that it has a classic Madagascan profile of good acidity and strong citrus flavours at the outset, finishing with a hint of red fruit. No floor polish, guaranteed.

In 2015, Mast hit a little bit of controversy, being accused of melting down industrial chocolate and passing it off as their own creation. According to Mast, they tested their techniques in the start-up phase with industrial chocolate, to help work out how chocolate was made, but it was never actually sold to the public. CEO Rick Mast famously invoked a quote often attributed to Mark Twain: 'A lie can run half way around the world before the truth gets its shoes on,' and dismissed the story as 'fake news'. Still, when did facts ever get in the way of a good rumour? Chocolate bluffers should put people right on this.

FRESCO

The USA has become something of a spiritual home to chocolate makers. It's possibly because of their relative proximity to where so many of the beans are grown, possibly because of the rise of artisan food producers across the country and, most likely, a combination of both.

On the opposite coast to Mast Brothers, Fresco is doing great things in the name of micro-batch production. You'll often hear food producers boast of their 'local, seasonal' credentials. Fresco can't claim local – they're in Lynden in Washington State, where there's not a whole lot (read 'zero') of cacao growing – but they're big on seasonal.

Each batch produced is to a different recipe, depending on the origin of the bean, the cocoa percentage, the roasting levels and conching time. These details are recorded on its highly detailed labels alongside the number assigned to that particular recipe. As cacao is subject to seasonal changes, Fresco will tweak the recipe to get the most out of their beans. As they say, 'We could never create every combination – but we can try.'

Beans are sourced from around the world – Venezuela, Madagascar, Papua New Guinea, the Dominican Republic and Jamaica to name but a few of the recent beans used. The chocolate is available via outlets around the world. One recent bar – recipe 217 – for example, was a well-received, Good Food Award finalist made of Chuao from Venezuela, 70% cocoa solids, dark roasted and a medium conching. Words like 'fig', 'coffee' and 'toast' would be good to use.

DUFFY'S

Cleethorpes, Lincolnshire. No, it's not the first place that springs to mind when you're thinking of chocolate but, for our purposes, that makes it all the more memorable, which is a very good thing.

Former Formula 1 engineer Duffy Sheardown trades as Red Star Chocolate but, perhaps wisely like other British chocolate makers (*see* below), he's now using his own name for what's becoming a highly acclaimed range of hand-produced bars. Sheardown's background is – somewhat improbably – motor racing, and he started making chocolate when he learned that, at the time, Cadbury's were the only people making chocolate from the bean in the UK. So he started experimenting and, over the next few years, became pretty good at it. He's still experimenting and still very hands on, tasting all through the production process, which is probably the only way you can be in these circumstances. His chocolate is sold by mail order, local suppliers, leading London retailers and at a lot of food shows and fairs, frequently by the man himself.

As you will know by now, small and independent is good, especially when the middleman is cut out. The best chocolate makers, you will say, are those like Duffy who work directly with the cocoa farmers, paying a premium for the beans which would otherwise go to you-know-who.

All the bars are single origin. Of particular interest is Duffy's Corazon del Ecuador bar. This translates as 'Heart of Ecuador' and Duffy's produces two versions with the beans: a 72% dark chocolate and a 43% milk chocolate. As you know – although a little revision never hurts – Ecuador beans make typically floral chocolate. Here, the dark chocolate has hints of orange blossom, the milk chocolate less so, but still with a pleasing citrus taste.

WILLIE HARCOURT-COOZE

You may have seen the irrepressible Willie on his TV show, *Willie's Wonky Chocolate Factory*, a fine watch about his struggle to be, at the time, the only bean-to-bar chocolate maker in the UK. He has taken the process one step further than most by actually owning a cacao estate as well. As it happens, this is in Parque Nacional Henri Pittier in Venezuela, meaning the acclaimed Chuao region is his neighbour.

Harcourt-Cooze replanted the estate with Criollo trees and suffered various trials and tribulations in setting up a factory in Devon, but now produces bars and his trademark cylinders of chocolate. The cylinders are of particular interest, from a bluffing perspective and otherwise, as they are 100% cacao; if you want to understand the tannin effect of chocolate – that mouth-drying feel – try a piece of 100% chocolate. The cylindrical shape, incidentally, is because Willie's original mould was a pipe.

The cylinders, available in various supermarkets, come in assorted varieties. They're designed to be used in cooking – grated over all kinds of food, blended into cakes or melted into hot chocolate, and there are recipes on the inside of the wrapper – and also have names that sound like something the bad guys deal in 1970s US police shows: things like Peruvian Black, Nicaraguan Black and, of course, Venezuelan Black. As well as the country of origin, Willie's labelling gives details of the more specific location the beans come from; for example, the Venezuelan Black is available in Hacienda La Cuyagua (with notes of fruit and nut), Carenero Superior (nut and spice), and Rio Caribe Superior (citrus) cylinders.

DAMSON

In a case of gamekeeper turned poacher, or very possibly vice versa, Damson is the chocolatey lovechild of Dom Ramsey, founder of Chocablog – one of the biggest and longest running chocolate blogs on the web – Cocoa Runners (a company dedicated to importing and supplying some of the world's leading bars to shops and cafes in the UK) and the World Chocolate Guide.

In 2014, Dom started experimenting with making his

own chocolate before starting Damson in 2015. Things started well – Dom's Madagascar 70% and Ecuador 70% bars both won bronze medals at the 2015 Academy Of Chocolate Awards, and Damson received a special 'One To Watch' award as well.

Sadly, in July 2016, Dom arrived at his Islington shop to discover the place engulfed in thick black smoke, from a fire caused, he believes, by a faulty extension lead. Facing a huge repair bill it looked to be game over but, chocolate lovers being the wonderful people they are, a crowdfunding campaign raised enough money to get Dom back on his feet.

Dom's little twist to the chocolate making formula is to age his for between two and four weeks after grinding to develop the flavours before tempering. We gather many do the same, as it can help produce a more consistent flavour, but few are as open about the fact as Dom. Thank you then, Dom, for some excellent bluffing information.

AMEDEI

You could easily hate Alessio and Cecilia Tessieri, the brother and sister behind Amedei. Not only do they make some of the best chocolate in the world, celebrated by chocolatiers, pâtisserie chefs and gourmets worldwide, but they get to make it in a ridiculously attractive factory in ridiculously attractive Tuscany – in Pontadera, near Pisa, to be exact.

Cecilia was a chocolatier. Alessio worked for the family food firm which makes pastry products. In the 1980s, he went to Venezuela where he began establishing relationships with local farmers. His relationships there have continued to develop, to the extent that they have access to Chuao (the celebrated plantation already mentioned once or twice). They also make a bar from Porcelana which is of particular interest to bluffers because it has lots of interesting facts and figures attached to it, and is expensive and rare. These pale Criollo beans – porcelana/porcelain, remember? – produce a slightly lighter bar, even with the 70% cocoa solids Amedei uses. There are only enough Porcelana beans worldwide to make some 3,000kg of chocolate every year. Amedei makes a third of that total – 20,000 50g bars to be precise – and each one is individually numbered. In terms of flavour, it's regarded as beautifully rounded, delicate, with subtle fruit and spice and a great lingering finish. While it is strongly suggested that you try this one, that information could probably save you about £10.

VALRHONA

Like Amedei, Valrhona has become a brand so synonymous with chocolate quality that pâtisserie chefs and chocolatiers will often make a point of citing the fact that their creations are made with chocolate from this particular maker.

It's a French company, this time: easily remembered, as the factory is located in the Rhône Valley (the alert bluffer will already have spotted the provenance of the name). Part of its fame has to do with its longevity; the company has been around in some form since the early

1920s – becoming Valrhona in 1947 – and was perhaps the first company to celebrate the potential joys of the 70% bar. It was certainly the first to produce single-estate 'Grand Cru' chocolates in 1986 with the launch of Guanaja – billed, rather oddly, as the 'bitterest chocolate in the world'.

By today's standards, this 70% bar of Caribbean origin is still great, but doesn't seem so bitter. As you'd expect from cocoa beans of Caribbean origin – you know, being an expert now – it covers all the main flavour profiles, from floral to fruity, nutty to toasty, spicy to smoky. Because of that, it's a very good one to, (some might say), 'show off with', but perhaps 'demonstrate your tasting prowess' is a more accurate way of putting it. Note that it's a very well-made bar, plus there are absolutely no wrong answers in terms of the flavour notes you suggest you detect.

MODICA

Those who know about these things (mostly fellow bluffers) say that the chocolate produced in a charming old baroque town in the south of Sicily is the closest it is possible to get to the original *xocoatl* made by the Aztecs. But Modica isn't an actual company making authentic chocolate; rather, it is an entire community dedicated to keeping alive ancient skills which have passed down the generations.

When the island was part of the Spanish Empire from the fifteenth to seventeenth centuries, it benefited from many of the exotic new foodstuffs being brought back by the *conquistadors* from South America. Cacao was the one that really caught the attention of the people of Modica, and the result is a 400-year-old tradition of producing very possibly the best chocolate in the world. This is one good reason to know about it, but the other is the priceless bluffing potential involved in the manufacturing process, known as 'cold-working'.

The main ingredients in Modican chocolate are hand-ground cocoa beans and sugar, and very little else except flavourings such as chilli pepper, cinnamon or vanilla. After toasting, the beans are ground with a stone known as a 'metate', then they are gently warmed and the sugar is added. But here's the important part (which you must commit to memory): the mix never goes above 40°C, so the sugar doesn't melt and retains a gritty, granular quality.

So, whenever you have the opportunity, pronounce authoritatively that the secret of Modican chocolate is in the cold-working, which, you might add, preserves more nutrients and flavours than modern methods of manufacturing. Nobody could possibly disagree with you and, should the subject come up, you might quote the Sicilian-born writer Leonardo Sciascia, who declared that 'Modican chocolate is unparalleled in savour, such that tasting it is like reaching the archetype, the absolute, and that chocolate produced elsewhere, even the most celebrated, is an adulteration, a corruption of the original.'

Either the Modicans really are onto something, or they're better bluffers than the Belgians.

SOME OTHER NAMES TO DROP

Pacari

Ecuadorian and developed as a sustainable model, where the makers work alongside local growers rather than shipping the beans worldwide. The chocolate is less processed than many bars, and produced at lower temperatures, which is said to protect the health benefits of cacao. The results are big in flavour but with a slightly grainy quality, rather than the sheen others strive for.

The Grenada Chocolate Company

You'll never guess where they're based… This is another cooperative idea, one of the few places anywhere to grow cacao and make chocolate at the same location. The chocolate is deservedly praised for its bold flavours, possibly due to the island's volcanic soil. Uniquely, all the company's machinery is powered by solar-electric energy; so while you're indulging yourself in some fine organic chocolate you can congratulate yourself that you're also doing your bit to save the planet. They even export by sailboat. Sadly one of the founders, Mott Greene, was electrocuted in 2013 while working on the solar-electric machinery to cool chocolate for overseas transport. Bluffers should be aware of this but ignore the irony.

Dormouse

Manchester's food reputation has grown considerably in recent years and, since May 2015, can even claim a microbatch bean-to-bar producer who hand sort their beans, roast, winnow, grind, refine and conch and temper in The Old Granada Studios, the former home of long-running soap opera *Coronation Street*. Bean to bar? Microbatching? It was never like that in Ena Sharples' day... Like Damson, they also age their chocolate, and like Damson, have already started clocking up the prizes at The Academy of Chocolate awards, including a gold for their 51.5% Milk Guatemala bar.

Hotel Chocolat

From small acorns, giant oak trees grow. In Hotel Chocolat's case, read 'acorns' as 'beans' and 'giant oak trees' as 'a huge retail business'. Since launching their first shop in 2004, founders Angus Thirlwell and Peter Harris have built an empire of 93 shops, cafés, restaurants and a hotel on their own St Lucia cocoa plantation. Obviously, success breeds a certain snobbery and backlash – it's the British way – but, as a seasoned bluffer, you can be happily contrary not least as, of late, Hotel Chocolat have greatly improved much of their offering, launching their own 'Supermilk' genre – milk chocolate with a very high percentage of cocoa solids – growing their own beans at their Rabot Estate and doing lots of ethical things to support cocoa farmers worldwide. They also keep waste to a minimum, even using the cacao shells to make a tea-like infusion. In short, it's very alright to like them. Even if they are annoyingly successful.

Love Cocoa

In a move seemingly designed for bluffers, Love Cocoa was founded by James Cadbury, the great-great-great-grandson of John Cadbury. Aware that his namesake firm wasn't terribly popular since selling out to mighty US food conglomerate Kraft, James also spotted a gap in the market for 'premium letterbox friendly chocolate gifts' and thus Love Cocoa was born. They produce bars using organic, fair-trade cocoa, ethically sourced from the Dominican Republic and Ecuador, and flavoured with items such as Maldon Sea Salt, Earl Grey tea, London-produced honey and mint from Basingstoke in Hampshire.

Rancho San Jacinto
Ecuador is clearly the place to be if you want to take your bean-to-bar-making to its most authentic form. Like Pacari, The Grenada Chocolate Company – and another Ecuadorian company, Kallari – Rancho San Jacinto grows the beans *and* makes the chocolate. The latter is a relatively new development, as before they'd ferment, dry and roast the beans and sell them on to other chocolate makers.

Amano
With packaging remarkably similar to Amedei, Amano isn't Italian but US-made near Salt Lake City. Scientist-turned-engineer-turned-chocolatier-turned-chocolate-maker Art Pollard took that final stage when he was disappointed with the chocolate available and thus decided to make his own. He's been one of the figureheads of the burgeoning US chocolate scene. The factory is of interest, too, as it's one of the highest in the world, 1,454m above sea level. Beans are sourced from

many different cacao-growing countries to make dark 70% bars as well as 30% milk bars.

Patric Chocolate

Sadly, not the name of the founder – although it is a deliberate, French-sounding misspelling of founder Alan McClure's middle name – Patric is another US bean-to-bar producer from Columbia, Missouri. Alan specialises in Madagascan beans, making bars of different percentages from the same source. He cites Valrhona as an inspiration after living in France for a year.

French Broad Chocolates

In the perhaps unlikely setting of Asheville, North Carolina – in the Blue Ridge Mountains (but not of Virginia) – husband and wife team Dan and Jael Rattigan make some of the US's best bean-to-bar products. They're so good, in fact, that you can even forgive them their ridiculously cool background story. The couple met at a wedding in 2003, travelled to Costa Rica – in a 40-foot vegetable oil-powered school bus that Dan had converted himself – and ended up running a café called Bread & Chocolate in a town called Puerto Viejo de Limon. They also bought an abandoned cacao farm. Flash forward a few years, and the couple – now plus kids – headed back to the US and opened French Broad Chocolates. They still own the farm and visit annually, getting ever closer to reviving it as a going concern. Hey, it's cacao. You can't rush cacao...

CHOCOLATE EARS

So, those were the chocolate makers, the people who take a bitter bean, do mad things to it for a few days and create the subject of this book. Remarkable. Now it's time to take a look at some of the world's leading chocolatiers.

The chocolatier is the next person in the production process/industry – or, certainly in some cases, the chocolate maker wearing a different hat – who takes the bar (or drop-sized pieces or tanker full of liquid, etc.) and turns it into their own creation. You remember them: the people who take couverture chocolate and fill it/tweak it/cover it in nuts/dip it/convert it to ganaches and truffles, and mould it into the shape of bunny ears at Easter (actually, not too many self-respecting practitioners of the art do the latter).

In order to taste examples from all the great chocolatiers of the world, you'd have to travel some 37,000 miles, consume nearly half a million calories and spend somewhere in the region of £147,000. Possibly. These figures are made up, but some people will believe anything. And anyway, there's no doubt a grain of truth in there somewhere.

In this section, you'll meet some of the finest chocolatiers on the planet who will, hopefully, leave you equipped to drop – to chocolate drop, in fact – some key facts into conversations. What finer way to trump another guest's expensive gift of handmade chocolates than to compare it to an even more obscure product from the other side of the world? Imagine the thrill of sampling a beautifully made ganache, allowing it to melt on your tongue, as your eyes moisten soulfully and you declare it to be 'marvellous… but perhaps not quite as good as the ones made by Aquim in Rio de Janeiro', or, 'This reminds me of a truffle I had in a little café in Waikiki.'

AQUIM

And talk of the devil…Aquim is a very good place to start. Not only is it fantastically obscure as far as the European market is concerned, but it's also been involved in some arguably pretentious designer pairings at its boutique and café on Avenida Ataulfo de Paiva, the main street of Rio's upmarket Leblon area, including a US$1,000, wave-shaped chocolate bar designed by curve-loving architect Oscar Niemeyer.

The chocolate business was set up by Samantha Aquim, whose father introduced her to imported Lindt chocolate as a child, but on the condition she let it melt in her mouth instead of chewing. Later, at a French cooking school, she was inspired by chocolatier Thierry

Alain and returned to Brazil determined to make her own chocolates using top-quality Brazilian cocoa.

You may have noticed that Brazil was omitted from an earlier chapter. That's because the industry was nearly wiped out by a fungus in the 1990s. However, with the support of people such as Aquim and growers experimenting with new trees and fusions of different cacao varieties, things are slowly – and literally – growing.

Aquim makes her very pretty creations with a 77% chocolate and presents them as if in a jewellery store. The Niemeyer partnership was, according to the chocolatier, like 'asking God to design you a chocolate bar'. Well, that might be over-egging the creation slightly, but it gives you some idea of how seriously chocolatiers take their art.

PAUL A YOUNG

Not Paula Young. Paul A Young. This name has popped up a few times so far, so make sure you get it right. He's a big personality, and not just in the chocolate world – a Yorkshire-born force of nature who's been at the forefront of the UK's chocolate revolution over the last few years.

A former pâtisserie chef whose experience includes a stint working for Marco Pierre White, Young opened his first tiny store in Islington in 2006. That was followed by a branch at the Royal Exchange in the City of London in 2007 and a much larger Soho shop in 2011. His cookery book, *Adventures With Chocolate*, won the Gourmand Cookbook Award for World's Best Chocolate Book in 2010.

The holder of many awards for his chocolates – for example, his salted caramels and 85% Raw Ecuadorian plain truffle won gold medals at the International Chocolate Awards in 2012 – Young is particularly famous for some rather unusual combinations of flavours, such as Stilton and port, Marmite (again), and pink peppercorn and saffron truffles. No, really. But with all those hundreds of flavour profiles, chocolate goes with a lot of things. And Paul A Young seems to be on a mission to test every single one of them. The aroma of chocolate in his shops is usually boosted by a bubbling vat of his award-winning hot chocolate and a platter or two of his celebrated, multi-flavoured brownies. It is, as a result, highly threatening to your willpower. Summer is a great time to visit – or pretend you've visited – as there are usually house-made chocolate ice creams and sorbets to be had.

WILLIAM CURLEY

Also threatening wallet, waistline and willpower is William Curley's Richmond (the south-west London one) boutique. Curley is a Scot who single-handedly undermines all those 'deep-fried Mars Bar' assumptions. Like Paul A Young, his background is in pâtisserie, having worked at the likes of Le Manoir aux Quat'Saisons and La Tante Claire. Unlike Young, Curley is still a pâtissier and his second, larger premises in London's Belgravia is a celebration of his skill in this field; there's also an impressive dessert bar there at weekends. Curley's Japanese wife, Suzue – also a pâtissière, as it happens

– has undoubtedly had an influence on the range of chocolates made with flavours such as Toasted Sesame and Japanese Black Vinegar.

He also has a concession in Harrods and has been voted 'Britain's Best Chocolatier' four times by the Academy of Chocolate. One of his most popular collections is the Nostalgia Range which takes sweet things familiar from a British childhood – Jaffa Cakes, Bounty-like coconut bars, marshmallow-filled Wagon Wheels, peanut-and-caramel-filled Snickers – and gives them an upmarket, gourmet twist, enrobed – now there's a good word for your chocolate discussions – in Amedei's finest couverture. And in case you were wondering, yes, William Curley is quite curly.

ARTISAN DU CHOCOLAT

We'll venture back around the world shortly, but British chocolatiers are definitely worth celebrating. And, although it sounds French, Artisan du Chocolat has been one of the leading lights in the industry since the shop opened in London in 2001.

The business was founded by Irish – you guessed it – pâtissier Gerard Coleman. After a stint at the Gramercy Tavern in New York (which also gave a Mast Brother his start, remember), Gerard trained with Belgian chocolatier Pierre Marcolini before returning to London.

His chocolates first appeared at Restaurant Gordon Ramsay – located just a short walk from the original Artisan du Chocolat shop. (Ramsay, by the way, refers to Artisan as 'the Bentley of chocolate'.) Heston Blumenthal then got in on the act, serving Gerard's tobacco chocolates as a post-dinner treat at The Fat Duck.

Perhaps the landmark year for Coleman and his company was 2003, when he created the liquid sea-salted caramels for Gordon Ramsay at Claridges. These have become a huge cult item and salted caramel has become surprisingly mainstream, as previously discussed. In 2007 Artisan started conching its own chocolate in-house from ground cocoa beans; it has a vast, state-of-the-art factory in Ashford, Kent.

As well as its flagship Chelsea store, Artisan du Chocolat has a second London shop in Notting Hill, concessions in Selfridges in London, Birmingham and Manchester, and a stall selling its most popular ranges, such as the jewel-like truffle Pearls, bars and filled chocolate disc 'O' selection (plus bags of 'seconds' – imperfect or damaged chocolates), at south London's Borough Market.

In addition to the single-source bars you'd expect, Coleman makes interesting flavoured bars, using ingredients such as Darjeeling or Matcha green tea. For those with dietary requirements, there are also sugar-free bars and even an almond milk bar for the lactose intolerant.

PIERRE MARCOLINI

Having referenced him above – and having also blithely dismissed the Belgians for their chocolate marketing ruse – another fine name to mention is Pierre Marcolini. He has 'haute chocolaterie' shops in Brussels, Liège and

Antwerp, offers 'Le Macaron du Mois' – 'The Macaroon of the Month' – and actually roasts his own beans.

Similarly to Aquim, the Brussels flagship store is like an expensive jeweller's. The packaging is also highly stylish – matt black with silver, and white labelling. Alongside the truffles, pralines, macarons and biscuits are *palets fins*, small squares of filled chocolate and Marcolini's own creation. 'My need to challenge conventions, question what I do and break new ground led to the creation of these chocolate squares that weigh barely six grams,' explains Pierre on his website, 'because our consumer codes have changed, too: more flavour, more texture, more finesse, more fullness and above all less heaviness.' You may wish to recall this next time someone gives you a square of filled chocolate that isn't from Marcolini. Flavours include Caramel Gingembre (yes, as you'd expect, it's ginger), Miel (chestnut honey), Caramel Beurre Salé (the inevitable salted caramel) and Caramel Fleur d'Oranger (Algerian orange blossoms). 'They are hollow. But not empty,' continues Marcolini. 'Empty is nothing, whereas the hollow is filled…' If you've perfected that middle-distance stare or the desired air of moist-eyed reminiscence, this is a line you may wish to consider delivering any time you eat a filled chocolate. Not least because no one will have a clue what you're going on about.

ORIOL BALAGUER

One of the most splendid names to mention is Oriol Balaguer. His food credentials are impeccable. Based in the foodie Mecca that is Barcelona, he is a second-generation pâtisserie chef who worked with elBulli's Ferran Adrià. In 1993, when he was only 23 years old, Oriol was named Best Spanish Artisan Confectionery Master.

Nine years later, he opened his Chocolate and Confectionery Studio in Barcelona where, in elBulli style, he brings together the familiar and unfamiliar in confections some – i.e., you – should describe as avant-garde.

His chocolates are shaped, appropriately enough, like the cocoa pod. That's possibly the last recognisable thing about much of his filled chocolate range. Dark chocolate is infused with raspberry. Balaguer's Mascleta chocolate – probably his signature – combines hazelnut praline and space dust/popping candy. Other flavours in his repertoire include an olive oil and white chocolate ganache, a black truffle and milk chocolate praline, Cava, and a chocolate filled with a ganache of crunchy toasted corn. You can buy a selection of 18 of his chocolates in a box marked 'My Obsession', which seems rather fitting in the circumstances.

RICHARD DONNELLY

Unlike Oriol, Richard Donnelly's career in chocolate wasn't predisposed. In fact, he was going to be a lawyer. However, an obsession with flavour saw him change tack and study chocolate making instead – as so many do.

After that, Donnelly, an American, worked at various European chocolate companies before returning to the USA and working with La Nouvelle Pâtisserie in San Francisco. He then tried opening a chocolate shop near Boston – using his mother's kitchen to make the chocolates – which was a failure, before reopening in Santa Cruz, California, a couple of years later.

In 1988 Donnelly became one of the first chocolatiers to offer fine chocolate in bar form, both as single varietal and flavoured. He makes fine chocolates in small batches, and the flavours offered now include almond, coffee, cardamom, Chinese five spice, rose, lavender, orange, fresh mint, assorted seasonal flavours and a best-selling chipotle variety, which was inspired by a customer requesting a spicy pepper chocolate. The vanilla ganache is highly acclaimed. He also produces a brownie mix that you can make up at home.

AND SOME OTHER NAMES TO MENTION

Rococo
Working in Harrods at the chocolate counter, the delightfully named London chocolatier Chantal Coady realised a few things. Chocolate shouldn't be stuffy and conservative. It should be fun and engage the senses. It could still have a sense of the traditional – see Rococo's Rose & Violet Creams – but it should be enjoyable. Three decades on she's been proved right, with three shops, multiple awards and the *Wall Street Journal* declaring Chantal as 'the founder of the New British School of chocolate'. Joanne Harris, the author of *Chocolat*, was an early customer, hence rumours that Vianne was based on Chantal.

T'a

Milan's T'a – it's the initials of brothers Tancredi and Alberto Alemagna – has an impressive food heritage. The family business dates back to their great-grandfather Gioacchino Alemagna who, after the First World War, built the company based, allegedly, on having invented panettone – although others refute that claim. Regardless, a chain of bakeries followed. Now, T and A are making chocolate – very good chocolate – such as their 66% flavoured bars like Szechuan pepper and Sicilian lemon.

Co Couture

Belfast is getting in on the chocolate thing thanks to Deirdre McCanny, who has a fine chocolate shop on Chichester Street in the centre of town (just a few doors away from Marks & Spencer, should you wish to give your comments that extra degree of conviction which, naturally, you do). It's a bright, modern shop with a couple of tables; they serve hot chocolate with home-made marshmallows.

The chocolates are beautifully displayed and as well as Deirdre's own bars (with a signature piece of edible gold leaf in one corner), there are filled chocolates – the dark chocolate praline is reportedly excellent; the whisky truffle is an award winner – chocolate honeycomb, popcorn and hazelnuts, as well as bars produced by other chocolate makers.

Chocko Choza

Chocko Choza in Coimbatore is regarded as India's finest chocolaterie. Managing partner Dhivya gave up a job with technology company Infosys to start the business with former engineer and old school friend Anbuchelvan. Neither knew anything about chocolate making when they opened; they just wanted to do something that nobody else was doing. They found chefs and researched their subject. Then they started with a honey-and-raisin chocolate and today have a range of some 60 different flavours and a team of 15 who all have a stake, John Lewis-cooperative-like, in the business. Ingredients are sourced from around the world for the chocolates, cakes and biscuits.

She Chocolat

'She' stands for 'spiritual human evolution', after the teachings of Bernie Prior, co-founder of the She Café. Such faith has been tested at this café and chocolaterie in Christchurch, New Zealand, which, nine months after opening in 2004, was destroyed by a fire and had to be rebuilt. As it happens, that put the team in good stead for the devastating Christchurch earthquakes that followed, when they suffered only minor damage. She Chocolate came about when Oonagh Browne started making treats – such as the Decadent Date – and selling them at a local farmers' market. The businesses merged and continued to expand with a mobile café – a converted 1947 London double-decker bus – and a hot chocolate bar at a local hotel. Flavours range from single origin truffles to more adventurous things such as lime and black pepper.

Brontie & Co

From a tiny factory in West Sussex in England comes Brontie & Co., which ticks all the boxes for certain people:

organic, vegan and artisan, following the philosophy 'eat from nature'. Using single origin Peruvian Criollo nibs, former corporate lawyer Brontie Maria Ansell grinds her nibs – single origin Peruvian Criollo nibs, to be precise – for three days, sweetens them with carob syrup and adds organic oils to flavour. As an experienced bluffer, you'll know about the health benefits of chocolate but Brontie, perhaps, has a decent claim on producing a bar that's as close to good for you as chocolate can get.

Stick With Me Sweets

The idea behind New York's Stick With Me, founded by head chef Susanna Yoon, was to allow all chocolate-lovers to access the kind of chocolates 'made with the same care and attention as those in Michelin-starred restaurants'. Located in Nolita ('North of Little Italy'), Susanna and her team make exquisitely detailed confections in small batches with painstaking detail and patience: their bon bons are hand-shelled and take three days to create, and each mould is individually polished to ensure each resulting confection has a beautiful shine. Fillings are all ethically sourced – naturally, in both senses – locally where possible, further afield if not. The results are little works of art.

Studio Chocolate

As if to prove the nationwide rise of good chocolatiers – the chocolate spread, perhaps? – along comes Ellie Wharrad and her highly artistic creations at Studio Chocolate in Nottingham. Shunning university for Le

Cordon Bleu, Ellie studied pâtisserie, completed a stage with Michelin-starred chef Sat Bains, and visited Brugge where she thought 'why is everything so brown?'. And thus was born Studio Chocolate, where Ellie handpaints her creations – inspired by art, space and music – and now also hosts classes and events. Oh, and makes pretty amazing cakes too.

'Hitting your audience in the cultural references is a strong weapon for any bluffer to keep in their arsenal.'

SELL, SELL, SELL

By now you will know more about the joys and benefits and other properties of chocolate. You know how to spot the good stuff – and make sure that people know you know – and how to dismiss the more low-grade bars and products out there except, of course, for the time you want to laugh them off as a guilty pleasure.

The trick is how to wax lyrical on the more popular end of the market – but the biggest trick of all is how the manufacturers seek to persuade us to buy their products rather than something else from those crowded, foil-wrapped displays.

As has been established, an holistic knowledge of chocolate history lends an air of authority to your chocolate-themed declarations, and that should, perhaps, extend to some of the more popular bars and products available. Hitting your audience in the cultural references is a strong weapon for any bluffer to keep in their arsenal, so you'll need to be able to reference a few key moments in advertising history and ensure that you're forearmed with some highly quotable information in the process.

FERRERO ROCHER

A classic of the 1990s, this infamous TV advert turned the Italian chocolate Ferrero Rocher into an overnight sensation. And it proved, not for the first time in advertising history, that something so bad – can improbably be very good (albeit for the wrong reasons).

Picture the scene. The camera swings into a black tie party, full of elegantly dressed, sleekly cosmopolitan guests as the plummy voiceover explains in dreadful English that 'the ambassador's receptions are noted in society for their host's exquisite taste that captivates his guests...' The ambassador nods, and a white haired butler enters the room, bearing a tray holding a pyramid of gold foil-wrapped chocolates to the demonstrable delight of all attending. 'Delicieux!'exclaims one badly-dubbed actress. 'Excellente,' declares an equally badly-dubbed actor before an attractive woman sidles up to the ambassador and purrs – in an accent that borders on comedy French – the now classic line: 'Monsieur, with these Rocher you are really spoiling us.'

The advert managed several things. It made a chocolate invented only a few years before in 1982 appear to be a long-established classic. And it ensured that, even a quarter of a century on, the arrival of chocolates at any social occasion is frequently met with the statement: 'Ambassador, you are really spoiling us...'

You, of course, will know that the 'Ambassador' was only ever addressed as 'Monsieur'.

The campaign added considerably to the Italian chocolatier's coffers. The chocolate contains wafer and hazelnut paste, which is unsurprising as it was a hazelnut spread – Nutella – that built the Ferrero family fortune. For maximum bluffing value, do ensure that you pronounce this brand as 'noo-tella' not 'nuh-tella': the former is the correct pronunciation, the latter is the more common, but most definitely incorrect.

To prove there is money in chocolate and nuts – or, indeed, noots – you may wish to point out that Michele Ferrero, the son of the founder, left an estate valued at around $23 billion when he died in 2015.

CADBURY'S FLAKE

'The crumbliest, flakiest milk chocolate in the world.'

Armed with your new-found knowledge, you could obviously criticise any chocolate that crumbles and flakes rather than snaps but, in the context of this series of – essentially – soft core ads from 1959 until the early 90s, that's possibly missing the point.

Cadbury's launched the Flake, the textured bar that also launched the 99 ice cream, in 1920 but it took several decades – and, arguably, a relaxing of moral standards (tut!) before these legendary advertisements appeared. In short, all featured a beautiful girl, usually wearing something flimsy or, in the case of the famous overflowing bath advert, nothing at all, slowly unwrapping and nibbling suggestively on the bar in question. Yes, indeed, no subtext there, none whatsoever.

You may wish to point out that one of the earlier Flake girls was model Catrina Skepper, an ex-squeeze of Prince Andrew, and that the model in the bath was *Vogue* cover girl Rachel Brown.

The jingle – the semi-bluesy, somewhat nonsensical 'only the crumbliest, flakiest chocolate tastes like chocolate never tasted before' – received a brief revival with smoky voiced chanteuse Joss Stone in 2007 before being shelved for good in 2010.

MILKY BAR

You can justifiably point out that white chocolate isn't technically chocolate, but don't let that get in the way of some useful chocolate advertising history and quotable trivia regarding this classic campaign from Nestle.

The mainly western themed ads featured a blond-haired boy in NHS spectacles, typically dressed as a cowboy who, at some point in the gripping narrative declared that 'the Milky Bars are on me!'

The first ad aired in 1961, starring Terry Brooks who earned the vast sum of £10 for his appearance – although he did get a pay rise for the second year and all the Milky Bars he could eat.

Also worth remembering are the words to the original jingle –

'The Milkybar Kid is strong and tough, and only the best is good enough,

The creamiest milk, the whitest bar, the goodness that's in MILKY BAR!!!'

– because these were changed to 'the good taste that's in Milky Bar' when it was pointed out that there really wasn't much goodness in something where sugar was the main ingredient.

On a similar note, Nestle announced in 2017 that they were increasing the amount of milk in the recipe, to make that the main ingredient. Given the name it's probably about time, to be fair.

MILK TRAY

One of the longest running products in the Cadbury range, Milk Tray was launched in 1915. It's a box of chocolates which, in the 1970s, was famous for two main reasons: the barrel shaped chocolate with an inedible lime filling (you may wish to speculate that it might arguably be the worst mass-produced chocolate in British history); and, mostly, its quite legendary advertising campaign featuring a James Bond-type figure in black who would stop at nothing – from avalanches to waterfalls, broken cable cars to heavily armed castles – to deliver a box of chocolates to a mystery woman. Why did he go to all this trouble? Couldn't he afford the postage? Well, we're asked to believe that he did it 'all because the lady loves Milk Tray'.

You might speculate drily on why he never stuck around for the thank you kiss or could be certain that she wasn't diabetic. One assumes it was to avoid the inevitable fall-out caused by the indigestible endurance test masquerading as a 'lime barrel'.

The campaign started in 1968, and ran for 15 years, with some six actors playing the hero.

You might also wish to point out that some of the ads were directed by Adrian Lyne, who also made 9 ½ Weeks, and thus has considerable history of mixing dodgy seduction techniques with food – also apparently known as 'sploshing' (but that's probably too much information).

ROLO

In the same advertising genre as Milk Tray – and, arguably Flake – Rolo has long demonstrated that chocolate and romance are natural bedfellows. This notion took a rather touching turn in the 1980s, when Mackintosh's milk chocolate covered caramels Rolos, were advertised with the tagline 'Do you love anyone enough to give them your last Rolo?'

The resulting commercials included one rather bleak narrative with acclaimed actor and playwright Patrick Barlow as a newlywed husband and his bride on a train where a 'loveheart' had been drawn in the condensation of the carriage window. As the honeymooners enter a tunnel there's only one Rolo left in the wrapper. When they emerge the husband is outraged to see that the Rolo packet is empty and his wife is contentedly chewing. Angrily, he wipes the heart from the window and turns away in disgust. It's not exactly Pinter, but it has a certain existential appeal. The rest of the ads in the campaign were less harrowing and proved that true love was in fact inextricably linked to the gift of the last Rolo. Obviously Nestle didn't agree, because when they bought the brand from Mackintosh the campaign was declared overly sentimental and it was abandoned in 2003. Bad mistake.

FUDGE

A finger of fudge is just enough to give your kids a treat.
A finger of Fudge is just enough until it's time to eat.
It's full of Cadbury goodness, but very small and neat.
A finger of Fudge is just enough to give your kids a treat.

While the finger of Fudge is still available, the advertising campaign is sadly no more: the notion of sugary snacks to tide the kids over until suppertime would cause justifiable concern in middle class kitchens throughout the nation.

It's rather a shame for, as jingles go, this was one of the more memorable ones – even if it contained a famously misheard lyric of 'peppery' rather than 'Cadbury' goodness. That, a primed bluffer might speculate, could make it far more acceptable to today's modern audience. After all, if salted caramel can be a world beating success, why not peppered fudge?

The song, as it happens, was based on an olde English folk song called The Lincolnshire Poacher (you may wish to note that this is also the name of a very good cheddar cheese) and the updated lyrics were written by Manfred Mann's Mike d'Abo.

YORKIE

A return to the 1970s – clearly the heyday of unhealthy advertising – for this (literal) slab of chocolate-based nostalgia.

The bluffing potential here is strong, mostly because like many of those mentioned here, the adverts haven't aged well. Such circumstances do, almost inevitably, lend themselves to contemplative facial expressions – a key part of your bluffing weaponry – as you wax lyrical on these changing times.

In this instance, it's no doubt a change for the better as this somewhat chauvinist campaign encapsulates, in just one minute, quite a lot of what was wrong with the 1970s, from its casual sexism to the literally jaw-breaking item it was selling.

The size of the Yorkie has shrunk over the ensuing years. It originally weighed in at a mighty 58g, came in six tooth-challenging chunks – marked Y, O, R, K, I, and E – and was advertised as the perfect snack to keep a gnarled trucker going all day, while he delivered whatever was on his trailer to wherever it was going, and simultaneously indulged in the lazy patronising of passing female drivers. Not forgetting, of course, that it was all to the tune of a very dodgy country and western 'song' that acknowledged the bar's teeth-challenging nature in lines such as 'good, rich and thick, a milk chocolate brick, each bite a chunky big mouthful.'

A new campaign launched in 2001 which didn't exactly alter perceptions, billed the now slightly smaller bar as being 'not for girls' which, unsurprisingly, went down like a ton of (rich, thick, milk chocolate) bricks. The current bar is still available but now weighs in at 46g, a 21% reduction on the original.

CARAMEL

And, finally, an honourable mention for the oddly attractive Caramel Bunny, an animated character voiced by Miriam Margolyes who advertised Cadbury's caramel-filled chocolate bar with the tag line 'take it easy'. In 2009, the bunny was voted the third sexiest cartoon character of all time after Jessica Rabbit (no relation, you may wish to point out at this point) and Betty Boop.

There's no point in pretending that you know everything about chocolate – nobody does – but if you've got this far and absorbed at least a modicum of the information and advice contained within these pages, then you will almost certainly know more than 99% of the rest of the human race about what chocolate is, how it is made, where it is made, and why it is eaten in such vast quantities throughout the world.

What you now do with this information is up to you, but here's a suggestion: be confident about your new-found knowledge, see how far it takes you, but above all have fun using it. You are now a bona fide expert in the art of bluffing about an ancient foodstuff with few rivals in its global appeal to people of all cultures, races and religions (especially religions) and which is more voguish today than at any time in its long and illustrious history.

GLOSSARY

Acosta's *Historie of the West Indies* This seminal tome by the sixteenth-century Spanish missionary and historian José de Acosta should be beside every chocolate bluffer's bedside, if only because it is thought to be the first time the word 'chocolate' appears in print. You will, of course, know that it was translated into English by Edward Grimstone in 1604. These minor details are important.

Aztecs The mighty empire that named a 1970s Cadbury's bar and held chocolate in such high regard that they used it as currency. Also the people who gave the world Montezuma, who gave us the idea of chocolate as an aphrodisiac. Possibly correctly, as it happens.

Baby Ruth A chocolate bar with arguably the most famous starring role in a Hollywood movie. It appeared in the swimming pool scene in the 1980 comedy *Caddyshack* where it was mistaken for a human turd.

Belgium Cunning country that somehow made people think they make the best chocolate in the world when, generally speaking, they don't. There are some exceptions – Pierre Marcolini, for example – but mostly they just employ fiendishly clever marketing.

Blooming A pooling of cocoa butter crystals – either as a result of poor tempering or because the chocolate has melted and solidified again and the cocoa butter has pooled rather than been evenly spread through the end product.

Bournville The model village near Birmingham – and later a chocolate bar – created as a workers' utopia by Quaker industrialist George Cadbury.

Cacao The tree that started it all, and still starts it all today. Also used to describe the beans before they get processed into what we now recognise as chocolate.

Cacao nibs The inside of the cacao bean and the bit we use to create all that delightful brown stuff.

Chocoholic An expression first used in 1961 in a Californian newspaper to describe a person who is addicted to chocolate. It was originally meant as a joke but has since entered the English lexicon.

Chocolate A product made – pretty much via alchemy with a scattering of miracle – from the fruit of the cacao tree. Or cocoa, depending on how you look at it.

Chocolate-box Adjective used to describe an image depicted in an idealised and airbrushed manner. Often used in the context of Christmas cards and, er, chocolate boxes.

Chocolate houses The British forerunners to gentlemen's clubs – no, not that sort. When chocolate came to Britain in the seventeenth century, it was initially the drink of the elite who got to drink it in dedicated chocolate houses while discussing politics and matters of the day – and probably England's incompetence at football, even though it had still to be invented.

Chocolate maker A person (or company) who takes the beans and turns them, via magic/hard labour/alchemy, into chocolate.

Chocolate teapot A derogatory expression used to describe someone or something not quite fit for purpose, as in: 'You're about as much use as a chocolate teapot (or fireguard/saucepan/kettle/soldier).' Similar to 'about as much use as a one-legged man in an arse-kicking contest', but not quite as entertaining in terms of mental imagery.

Chocolatier A person who takes already-prepared chocolate and turns it into their own creations, such as ganaches, truffles, puddings, etc.

Chocolatl (or *chokolatl* or *cacahuatl* or probably many other words that look like the board in an episode of

Countdown). Alternative spellings/derivations of the drink made from the cacao bean.

Cocoa The powder that's made from cacao beans, as familiarised by hundreds of Enid Blyton tales. Can also be used as the name of the tree and the beans rather than cacao – cocoa, that is, not Enid Blyton – particularly if you're eager to demonstrate your superior knowledge. Which you are.

Conching You've fermented, dried, roasted, cracked, winnowed, ground and mixed. Now you conch. The conching machine is a big mixer – originally with shell-shaped paddles (*concha* in Spanish, hence the name). The purpose: reduce the particle size further, coat each particle with cocoa butter, remove some of chocolate's less appealing qualities – bitterness, acidity, etc. – caramelise the sugars and develop the desirable flavours.

Cortés, Hernán The Spanish explorer who, apparently, looked a lot like a banished god (*see* 'Quetzalcoatl' on page 122). Now, there's a chat-up line. He also introduced cacao to the Spanish court and thus Europe.

Cracking Also known as 'fanning'. Does what it says: the roasted beans are cracked, to separate the shell from the kernel to get at the all-important cacao nib inside. Can also be used to describe the delicious end product (or puddings).

Criollo One of the three main varieties of cacao bean, and the hardest one to grow. The name translates as 'of local origin' and it makes up only around 5% of the world's cacao trees. Do not expect to see this in your local garden centre any time soon. It is regarded as the best bean, with a strong aroma and very little bitterness. Add several pounds – in cash terms – any time you see this on a label.

Drying Stage two in the frankly ridiculously complex chocolate-making process. This stage removes 94% of the beans' moisture content and half the weight. Should be done naturally; sometimes done with wood fires, which can leave you with a smoky-tasting end product.

Fanning *See* 'Cracking'.

Fermenting The first stage of chocolate making, an essential stage that reduces the beans' natural bitterness. Cacao pods are broken open and the seeds are laid out on leaves and left in the heat to ferment. How they discovered this is lost in the annals of time. When the pods are opened, they reveal cacao seeds. After fermentation, they're known as cacao beans.

Forastero One of the three main varieties of cacao bean. The name means 'foreigner' because it is thought to have originated in the Amazon Basin. The most common cacao variety, making up around 80% of the world's cacao trees.

Fry, Joseph The Quaker businessman acknowledged as the inventor of the chocolate bar. Bless you, Mr

Fry. Discovered that by blending powdered cocoa with cocoa butter and sugar, you could make a paste that could be easily shaped, creating a bar that could be eaten and not turned into a drink. Called the resulting product *'chocolat délicieux à manger'*, but we'll forgive him for that.

Grinding As it sounds. After fermenting, drying, roasting, cracking and winnowing the nibs, they are ground in Suchard's invention, the mélangeur.

van Houten, Conrad Inventor of the cocoa press, the device that separates cocoa butter from chocolate liquor and thus leaves behind cocoa powder, in a process named, sort of in his honour, as Dutching.

Kibbling *See* 'Winnowing'.

Lindt, Rodolphe (or Rudolf, or Rudolphe, depending on your preference). The Swiss inventor of conching although, according to chocolate-making legend, he discovered the process and the benefits completely by accident when an employee left a machine running overnight.

Mayans Behind the Olmecs and ahead of the Aztecs, the culture to fully embrace *xocoatl* and its health benefits and to make it an integral part of their society and religion. The spirit lives on in everyone who's ever eaten chocolate, rolled their eyes heavenward and exclaimed, 'Oh God…'

Mélangeur The machine that combines cocoa paste and sugar into a smooth blend, invented by Philippe Suchard (*see* page 123).

Mixing After fermenting, drying, roasting, cracking, winnowing and grinding, the chocolate paste is mixed. This is where most of the other ingredients – sugar, milk or vanilla, for example – are added. The chocolate is passed through a roll refiner or ball mill to reduce the particle size of the cocoa mass, helping disperse the cocoa butter evenly. Seriously, how did we discover this?

Montezuma The Aztec emperor who, as well as possibly demonstrating cacao's aphrodisiac/Viagra-esque properties, decided that Spanish explorer Hernán Cortés was banished god Quetzalcoatl returning, gave up the secret of cacao and put in motion his own death and the end of his civilisation. Whoops.

Nestlé, Henri The German chemist who worked out how to powder milk, which Daniel Peter then used to invent milk chocolate. Clearly employed a better PR agency than Daniel Peter.

Olmecs The people who started it all. As well as being the first on record to have consumed chocolate, they're also easily remembered for their love of organisation – inventing zero, calendars and, quite possibly, a written language. They lived from around 1200BC until 400BC and died out for reasons unknown. Or evolved into today's HMRC.

Peter, Daniel Another Swiss chocolate maker who first combined powdered milk and cocoa to create milk chocolate. Lost the PR battle to his neighbour, Henri Nestlé.

Quakers The religious group who took chocolate to their hearts due to its health benefits and lack of alcohol. Chocolatiers would soon rectify that with the invention of chocolate liqueur a few years later.

Quetzalcoatl Not another name for the drink but the god who the Toltecs believed had given man the gift of cacao and, as a result, was banished by the other gods. If someone's ever pinched your last Rolo, you can probably sympathise.

Roasting You've fermented and dried your beans. Now you have to clean them and roast them at 120–160°C for, typically, 10 to 35 minutes depending on what flavour you desire. It's alchemy, I tell you. It's alchemy. Someone sold their soul for this...

Rowntree, Joseph The third of the UK's leading Quaker chocolate industrial types.

Snickers Supposedly the best-selling chocolate bar of all time, introduced to the world in 1930 by Mars. It was named after the Mars family horse. For some reason it was rebranded as a Marathon bar in the UK until 1990.

Suchard, Philippe The man who took what Joseph Fry had learned about mixing ingredients to make bars and automated it, with his invention, the mélangeur.

Tablettes de chocolat The French expression for a rippling six-pack on a particularly toned example of Gallic manhood. (Sounds better than a *paquet de six*.)

Tempering You've fermented, dried, roasted, cracked, winnowed, ground, mixed and conched. Now you temper by pouring the chocolate onto a cool marble slab. The cooler outer edges are brought back into the middle of the chocolate. As the chocolate cools, the fat starts to crystallise. This mixing process spreads the fat crystals through the finished chocolate.

Theobroma cacao The Latin name for the cacao tree. It translates as 'food of the gods', so it's probably fair to say that Carl von Linnaeus, the eighteenth-century Swedish scientist who gave the tree this name, was a fan.

Toblerone One of many Swiss chocolatey gifts to the world, the distinctive pentahedron-shaped chocolate bar was created by confectioner Theodor Tobler in Bern, Switzerland, in 1908. Still made to the original recipe, it is a unique mix of chocolate, nougat, almonds and honey. The image of a bear (Bern's mascot) is hidden within the iconic Matterhorn logo on every bar (and frequently features in lists of 'cool hidden symbols'). This is bluffing gold. Also be aware of the outcry as the famous triangles were infamously downsized in 2016.

Trinitario One of the three main varieties of cacao bean, which makes up some 15% of the world's cacao trees. A hybrid of the other two beans, Criollo and Forastero, it was created on Trinidad – hence the name – after a hurricane wiped out the island's Criollo plantations, and makes a very fine chocolate.

White chocolate Not technically a chocolate at all because it contains no cocoa solids – just a minimum of 20% cocoa butter.

Winnowing Also known, brilliantly, as 'kibbling'. It's the application of air to blow away the outer shell of the cracked cacao beans, leaving you with the nibs.

Xocoatl Possibly the original name of the drink made from the cacao bean. Or possibly not. It translates as 'bitter water' which is, apparently, a fair reflection on the bitter, grainy, fatty, actually-probably-quite-unpleasant liquid consumed by the Olmecs, Mayans and Aztecs.